Just in time to serve the huge number of middle-aged children with aging parents. Whether you already are the family caregiver in charge, or might have that responsibility in the future, *The Unexpected Caregiver* offers information that is practical, sensible, and wise.

Connie Goldman, author,
The Gifts of Caregiving: Stories of Hardship, Hope, and Healing

Kari Berit's concise but engaging style delivers the kind of information that I need as I care for my aging parents, but in a way that is lively and heartfelt.

Paul Krause, CEO, Story Circles International Inc.

Kari's book offers a wealth of information and ideas for assuring that not only my own family, but those I work with everyday, can provide the best solutions for their parents.

Kyle R. Nordine, President and CEO,
Northfield (MN) Retirement Community

Kari Berit has written a comprehensive and useful guide to caregiving for the many boomers who will bear the difficult and yet noble role of caring for their aging parent(s). I highly recommend this book.

Paul D. Nussbaum, Ph.D., Clinical Neuropsychologist and
Adjunct Associate Professor, Department of Neurological Surgery
University of Pittsburgh School of Medicine

A splendid treasure chest of practical ideas that will help ease the stress of caring across generations.

Pat Samples, author, *Daily Comforts for Caregivers*

I am delighted with your message to an important group of people (the adult children of elders) who have incredible influence on the parents. You have a wonderful way of coming across to people with an honest, realistic message and in a conversational tone. Good for you.

Bruce Roberts, co-author,
I Remember When: Activities to Help People Reminisce

Kari Berit has spent her career searching for better ways to enrich lives of the elderly. Kari's advice for those of us who care for elderly loved ones is priceless.

Mike Eden, President, The Eden Group, Wilson, WY

A **Attainment Company, Inc.**
Verona, Wisconsin

[handwritten inscription:] 20. aug 2008
Ginger —
yeah, to reconnecting.
Blessing *[signature]*

The Unexpected Caregiver

How Boomers Can Keep Mom & Dad Active, Safe and Independent

kari berit

Act Your AGE
Smarts
™

Act Your Age
Smarts Act Your Smarts™, Age in Motion™ and age-assertive™ are registered trademarks of Kari Berit Presents, Inc.

Some of the basic principles in this book were first explored in the Active Seniors columns written by Kari Berit for *Creative Forecasting* magazine, Creative Forecasting, Inc., PO Box 7789, Colorado Springs, CO 80933-7789.

The Unexpected Caregiver:
How Boomers Can Keep Mom & Dad
Active, Safe and Independent
by Kari Berit

Editor: Dick Schaaf
Designer: Kirsten Ford, Focus Design

ISBN: 1-57861-606-9

An Attainment Company Publication

Printed in the United States of America.

Attainment Company, Inc.

PO Box 930160
Verona, WI 53593-0160
1-800-327-4268
www.AttainmentCompany.com

Kari Berit
PRESENTS
speaker. author. consultant.

PO Box 2
Red Wing, MN 55066-0002
www.UnexpectedCaregiver.com
www.KariBerit.com

To all Boomer caregivers who are
willing to take on this role . . .
and our parents:
You're the reason
we've had the occasion
to think this through.

Table of Contents

A Personal Approach To Caregiving

By Marge Engelman, Ph.D.
Author, *Aerobics of the Mind*

I have known Kari Berit for more than 15 years, first as a student in a class I taught at the University of Wisconsin, Madison, and since then as a professional colleague. Her enthusiasm is contagious. Her caring heart is huge. Her desire to share her experiences and knowledge knows no bounds.

For all these reasons and more, this book, *The Unexpected Caregiver*, is especially relevant for the Baby Boom Generation. Kari is a Boomer: She knows this turf. She has been both a professional consultant and a family caregiver. She writes for people who devote their lives to working with older adults, even as she has devoted her own life to working with her parents and extended family.

You will quickly sense that for Kari, caregiving is very personal. Her experiences with her own parents and with many others in senior centers, assisted living facilities, and nursing homes provide her with both simple, practical ideas and outright gems of wisdom. Her casual style of writing and understated sense of humor will draw you in. You'll come to recognize those proverbial elephants in your living room, but you'll also see the value of what she's recommending and find yourself thinking, "That makes good sense."

There are chapters here with insights about the issues that both divide and link generations, chapters chock full of good ideas about how to communicate, chapters with encouragement. My favorite is the chapter on children's books: It's a delight – a wonderfully gentle way to focus on attitudes about aging.

Not so long ago, there was little talk in my professional world about family caregivers. The focus was on the older person, period, and what we had to do for professionals addressing their needs. Thank goodness, we are now realizing that you, the family caregiver, are an increasingly key element in the care and support your parents receive.

You will find this book readable, enlightening, encouraging, perhaps a lifesaver for you as you walk your path. You may indeed be an "unexpected" caregiver. But know that you are needed, and valued, and admired for all that you do.

INTRODUCTION

Do We Really Have To Parent Our Parents?

By Dick Schaaf

You're a Boomer (so are we) – one of 78 million members of America's fabled Baby Boom Generation. You grew up in the '50s, '60s, '70s and '80s. Remember Nam, or at least its aftermath. Oil shocks. The advent of personal computers, and front-wheel-drive cars, and lots and lots of credit cards.

You've struggled through it. Stepped up to the challenges. Settled down and raised a family – maybe more than one, if lasting relationships have eluded you. Built some form of career or work history. Started looking ahead to a vague and mystical land called "retirement."

It's looking promising. The kids, if you had kids, are growing up, hopefully maturing, soon to be (or already) moving out and moving on with their own lives. They need you less. You need less. That creates a pool of "more" (especially more time and money) that you can start thinking about tapping for yourself. Time to travel, time for hobbies, time with friends your own age, just time off. Plus, the money to fund that time.

And then, when you least expect it, mom and dad (remember them?) re-enter your life. Or at least one of them does. In the pages that follow, we'll refer to your parents in the plural, for simplicity's sake, though we know your caregiving may be focused on only one of them. Through the wonders of medicine, their generation is living longer than ever before. And while that's mostly good, you're just beginning to discover there may be a price to pay.

They need to maintain their physical health. They need to maintain their emotional health. They need to maintain their lifestyle, and all the "stuff" that goes with it. When they can't do that maintenance for themselves, somebody else is going to have to step in and help them do it. Is that you?

Maybe you've starting asking yourself questions. Maybe you've been pretty good at avoiding them. But they're out there, lurking …

How long can they keep up with the house they're in?

Should they still be climbing stairs, climbing on ladders, shoveling snow, gardening in the heat?

How long can they keep driving safely?

What happens when they can't?

Are they eating right – or even regularly?

Are they taking their pills?

Are they getting forgetful – or is that the start of Alzheimer's?

How's their money holding out?

Do they understand their options for things like Medicare, Social Security, their supposedly "reliable forever" pension plans?

Are they vulnerable to direct-mail scams? Door-to-door scams? Identity theft scams? Unscrupulous TV preachers?

How are they coping with the steady loss of their siblings and their friends, the people they used to work with or play with?

Have they thought about the legacy they want to leave – to their children and perhaps to the community as well?

Do they have a will? A durable power of attorney? A healthcare directive? A funeral plan?

What – if anything – do they want done if and when something eventually happens to them?

And the biggest question of all: How much of that do they expect *you* to do?

So many questions. In an ideal world, you've identified at least some of them and sat down with mom and dad to talk things through. You've worked with your parents to explore issues, make plans, draft documents, and prepare for – ugly but unavoidable thought coming – their deaths.

In An Ideal World

In the real world, which is where most Boomers live, this stuff has been out there like a pile of snow on a low-hanging tree branch. If you're reading this book, odds are one day, not so long ago, you walked under that branch, mostly unsuspecting, and that load fell on you. Since then, nothing has been the same.

We chose the title of this book based on our own experiences as Boomers increasingly involved in the lives of our parents. For Kari Berit, the transition to caregiver was far from unexpected. She planned for it. She prepared for it. Truth be told, she saw it coming for years.

Whether your transition is equally planned or totally a matter of reacting to events (the latter is far more likely, I suspect), her preparation – both personal and professional – is about to pay huge dividends for you. Since 2002, Kari has been writing the Active Seniors column for *Creative Forecasting* magazine, a national journal for activity and recreational professionals. Her particular audience is the activity directors in care facilities who work with older adults to keep them as physically and mentally and emotionally healthy as possible.

My major contribution to this book, other than wordsmithing, is recognizing that we Boomers can benefit from the ideas Kari has been sharing with these caregiving professionals – so we can keep our parents out of those facilities for as long as possible, or help them adjust to that very different lifestyle when it becomes necessary.

This book is an anthology, but one step removed from its roots. It's composed of ideas, originally intended for professional caregivers, that we've reworked to fit the realities we Boomers face in trying to do some of the same things for our parents that professionals do, but without the education, training, experience and institutional support on which they can draw. (It's worth noting that we do have some advantages the pros don't: We know our parents, and we don't have to deal with the restrictions of facility-based care.)

Some people are beginning to refer to this as "parenting our parents." I think there are good and bad sides to the phrase:

◉ It's good in the sense that a parenting relationship involves care-giving, guidance, nurturing, emotional support, and a selfless commitment of time and energy over an extended period of time.

🌀 It's bad in the sense that it also implies a relationship of unequal partners: strong parents who know best, and protect weak and ignorant children from themselves and the world around them.

There's no avoiding the phrase (or the reality it describes), but I'll offer a specific perspective on it. When we parent children, they start from a position of ultimate weakness and progress to independence. For us, *as the parents*, "letting go" becomes the flashpoint as our urge to nurture and protect comes into increasing conflict with our children's push to break free and establish their independence.

If we're now going to refer to parenting our parents, we have to accept that the dynamic is flowing in reverse: Our parents start independent and will understandably struggle to maintain that independence as long as they can in the face of conditions that will gradually – or suddenly – erode their ability to do things for themselves. For us, *as their children*, the new flashpoint is "taking hold" of various aspects of their lives, but only if and as they need us to.

To help you in that context, we've organized this book in sections, clustering ideas drawn from Kari's columns around common themes in areas where you might unexpectedly need to take hold. You don't have to explore this book linearly, starting at page 19 and reading straight through to page 160. You might, in fact, want to flip through the section headings to find those that seem closest to the caregiving relationship you have, or expect to have, with your parents, and start there.

Here's something to know as you do so:

🌀 The first chapter in each three-chapter section deals with a significant issue you'll face as a caregiver: communicating effectively, keeping your parents mentally fit, encouraging them to stay socially active and not isolated at home, supporting their spiritual needs late in life.

🌀 The middle chapters offer support for you as a caregiver while you're working with your parents: meshing your communication styles, playing together, scrapbooking and preserving family stories, and using music to soothe or energize.

⊚ The third chapter in each cluster focuses on a tactic or activity you can do with your parents (adjusting your level of involvement to what they actually need): using children's books to introduce tough issues, getting them out walking, encouraging them to be involved as mentors, perhaps writing a children's book of their own as a family legacy, and figuring out who they want to receive their stuff when they're gone.

In the final chapter, Kari takes on one of the biggest elephants in anyone's living room: the complex relationships among family members, especially your siblings, and how to keep those linkages from being overwhelmed – or broken – by the stresses of caregiving.

Our goal is to give you a wide variety of practical ideas and sources of support. Not all of them will fit you, your parents, or the particular realities of the situation in which you find yourselves. But don't discard an idea as unworkable or "too out there" just because it doesn't fit the past relationship you've had with your parents.

Caregiving changes a lot of things – for them and for you. It has its trials and traumas. But it has its rewards, too. This may indeed be an unexpected role for you, one you're anything from committed to reluctant to take on. But it's a role that can help you deepen the relationship with the people who once meant everything to you: your parents.

Unexpected or not, give it a shot.

Dick Schaaf is Creative Director of Kari Berit Presents; on his own, he has written, co-written, ghosted or wordsmithed 18 books.

Challenges For Family Caregivers

SECTION 1

Caregiving absolutely requires active communicating. No matter how early or advanced their need, and how strong or nonexistent your past relationship, you and your parents must find common ground on which to exchange information, share emotions and move forward in the face of new challenges.

It's not about being right or wrong. Or taking charge. Or maintaining control. It's about getting past all the deep fears and fragile feelings, the things not said, the bright memories and the bittersweet ones, and coming to terms with the months and years that lie ahead.

They may be tough years. Trying years. Perhaps ultimately painful and tragic years. But they also can be years that call to something deep inside, resonating to chords only parents and their children can hear. Years that can leave you with a richness, a rightness, and a depth of love and satisfaction that lives on long after your parents are gone.

It starts with just communicating, however easy or awkward that may be. In this section, I'll help you focus on the underlying intergenerational issues that spawn so many elephants in so many living rooms. I'll examine some communication skills that can make this unexpected caregiver relationship more comfortable and more productive – for everyone involved. And I'll show you how simple books written for children have the power to open up resilient lines of communication that help the family come to terms with what's happening with mom and dad.

CHAPTER 1

Forging New Connections: Parents And Their Adult Children

Many of today's Baby Boomers are finding themselves pulled into a caregiver role with their aging parents – a role neither generation is prepared for. To make this new relationship take hold and become productive, ideally enjoyable, for adult children and their senior parents alike, two very different frames of reference will need to find some common ground on which to meet and interact.

And as both your parents and you probably remember only too well, that kind of interaction hasn't always been easy. Or peaceful. Or even possible.

No matter how calm or turbulent your communications with your parents may have been in the past, today you both need to be able to move forward and focus on their new realities. The issues of aging and the decisions that will need to be made toward the end of your parents' lives are complex. If you hope to play a positive role in them, it will help to start by acknowledging that you and your parents are coming to this new relationship with very different mindsets.

Boomer Basics

Let's start with what we see in the mirror. After all, we're Boomers. Where else would we start?

The easiest mistake to make is to assume that everybody who falls within the borders of the Baby Boom Generation – born between 1946 and 1964 – tends to think and act alike. Boomers constitute about a quarter of America's population. It's absurd to think that 78 million people are out there marching in lockstep. There are some basic distinguishing characteristics: comfort with change, a willingness to experiment and learn, a strong materialistic streak – often coupled with a deep reservoir of idealism. But there are significant differences among us as well.

The major divide within our generation is based in large part on how we experienced some of the key events of our youth, adolescence and early adulthood. In *New Passages* (1995: Random House), author and life-cycle expert Gail Sheehy splits us right down the middle chronologically:

🌀 Leading-edge Boomers, those born between 1946 and 1955, she labels the "Vietnam Generation." We'll accept the split, but use Leading-edge to refer to this half.

🌀 Those born between 1956 and 1965 Sheehy calls the "Me Generation." Cultural historian Jonathan Pontell has a term I like better: "Generation Jones," or "Jonesers." That's what we'll use.

I'm a Joneser – born in 1963, at the tail end of the Baby Boom. Dick Schaaf, my editor and wordsmith on this project, is Leading-edge – born in 1949. We're good examples of the bookends within which Boomers fall.

I remember where I was when the Challenger went down. Dick remembers where he was when John F. Kennedy was shot. I remember ice skating to "American Pie" and wondering "what's this Don McLean guy singing about?" I understood it to be a sort of sad song about death and being young and driving a Chevy to the levee. We had a Chevy – a paneled station wagon. And I did drive it to a levee once while growing up. But that's not at all what the song's about. Dick knew not only what it was about, but who. (All I knew is my feet were freezing, and my older sister, Anne, was getting the cute guys, and I was skating alone.)

Leading-edge Boomers were the trend setters. They turned the world on to Elvis and the Beatles, pushed for equality between the sexes and the races, learned how to tap mom and dad for spending money that fueled rapid growth in everything from the auto industry to shopping malls, and made a fetish of seeing themselves in the cultural spotlight.

They also joined in to demonstrate for civil rights, protested the war in Vietnam, burned bras and draft cards, and generally decided – from lots of "right there on the six o'clock news" experience – to distrust most political and government institutions.

We Jonesers occupy the shadowed ground between Leading-edge Boomers and their children, misfit Generation X, described by the online encyclopedia Wikipedia as people who believe "anything is possible, as long as you're willing to throw enough money at it." Even though I'm closer in age to the Xers, I identify more with the Leading-edge.

When people say Boomers, they're usually describing attributes of the Leading-edge. But that misses half the generational mindset. Perhaps because I am one, I think Jonesers tend to get lost within the larger label. But, like most Jonesers, I'm really not interested in taking sides.

Speaking as a Joneser to those on the Leading-edge, we're thankful for your hard work – and hard heads. Mostly, we're comfortable tagging along, sometimes following in your footsteps, sometimes rejecting your lead and charting our own course. But let's all agree to recognize that we're not all alike.

Before They Were Mom And Dad

Our parents are divided by a similar generational split. My parents are members of what Sheehy labels the "Silent Generation." Born between 1930 and 1945, these are the "duck and cover" kids who grew up initially with no family TV; later a big monster console black-and-white full of mysterious tubes. (In *their* childhood, as Peter Falk tells his grandson in *The Princess Bride*, television was called books.)

Dick's parents come from the generation before that (those born between 1914 and 1929), which Sheehy labels the "World War II Generation." As children, this generation grew up through World War I, Prohibition, the Depression and the lead-up to the Second World War. They remember turmoil and sacrifice and insecurity. But they also remember constant progress and improvement, both in their world and in their personal lives.

I remember working with independent residents of a senior community in Janesville, Wisconsin. The women fell mostly into this World War II Generation, and they'd plainly seen their share of pain and turmoil. But what they most relished was retelling stories of simple things. What they cooked, especially when there wasn't much in the pantry. How they turned old clothes into something new and different. How they ironed their sheets, napkins and sometimes even underwear. (Most of the time, I can't find my iron, and I go to extremes to not have to iron a thing.)

For both these parent generations, life was less complicated by stuff and technology. My Dad's family took "Sunday drives," spent time with their grandparents, and learned to greet guests, then excuse themselves to their rooms, going from "seen and not heard" to totally invisible. So did Dick's.

Interestingly, though my Dad is on the parent side of the generational divide, and Dick is coming to this as a Boomer, they have a lot of common experiences. Both remember their families getting their first TVs. Both were about nine at the time. Dad's favorite show: "Howdy Doody." Dick's: "Rin Tin Tin." Both their moms stayed at home, cooking, cleaning, keeping house, baking cookies (from scratch) for after-school snacks, raising kids. Both families always ate dinner together. After meals, both helped do the dishes. In a sink.

Often, they learned to do for themselves, or do without. Over the course of one summer, my Dad and his sister and brother made an army of soldiers out of clay, marching them around the porch. "If we didn't have toys, we made them from what we found," my Dad often tells me. His second wife (my Mom died in 2002) adds, "We really treasured our toys, because we had so few." Dick remembers sharing a bedroom with two brothers – and fitting everything they had, clothes and toys, into one small closet.

For both Dick and my Dad, it's difficult to watch their grandkids step over the mass of toys they simply take for granted. For each in his own way, that common experience of (and appreciation for) scarcity is common ground on which they can build caregiver relationships, my Dad with his children, Dick and his wife with their parents.

Appreciating The Differences

It's easy to say that the two halves of the Boomer generation and the two parent generations that birthed them come at things in uniquely different ways. But we need to be aware of those differences, because they can easily become divisive issues. We need to find a balance between having all the toys we want and treasuring a few toys; between maintaining old things and updating to newer. Expect that to be a recurring theme as you work with your parents in a care-giving role.

When my husband, Eric, and I moved in to share a house with my Dad, we had some major cleaning to do. I'll never forget finding a six-year-old piece of turkey in the freezer. We all laughed about the protective value of freezer burn … and then I went to throw it away.

"No," said my Dad. "Don't throw it. It's probably still okay."

He wasn't kidding. He cooked that old piece of turkey and ate most of it, insisting all the way, "It's not great, but it's okay." He takes the same approach with ketchup bottles. When they start looking all crusty and gross (and empty), we start looking for the recycle tub. My Dad adds a little water and *voila*: more ketchup.

When our washing machine quit, Eric and I looked into energy-efficient replacements that might have cost a little more, but would have been better for the environment. Dad said, "Let's just get my father's old one before we sell the house; that one is free." The way he was raised, free now was better than saving in the long run. As for the environment, you could probably argue that, simply by not tossing that old machine, Dad also was being environmentally conscious.

Both my Dad and I graduated from St. Olaf College in Northfield, Minnesota, some 25 years apart. My Dad worked for the family business in the summer so he could pay for his year of college. I knew what I could earn in a summer wouldn't come close to touching my tuition, so I took out loans.

Now you have to know that my Dad can drive me absolutely nuts when every little bit of everything has to be saved for later. But that's how he was taught by his mother. Some of that training he passed on to me, but I also grew up in a world of throwaway products and credit cards. We didn't need to wash and reuse, so often we don't. And when we can't afford to pay for something, we have those magic pieces of plastic.

My Dad has never carried credit-card debt at 18-percent interest. I have, but I'm pleased to say I no longer do.

Something To Talk About

As our parents begin to sense that their futures will not continue to stretch indefinitely, it's natural to begin to look back to the past. This can be a valuable starting point for the conversations that need to happen between the generations. In the stories you and your parents remember – often in very different ways – you can begin to develop a compatible frame of reference. By the way, working through enduring memories of the past is also a terrific way for your parents to maintain mental fitness.

We'll talk about storytelling in Chapter 4, and at greater length in Chapter 14. For now, as you look for ways to start productive conversations with your parents, ask yourself which stories you want to remember 20 years from now – especially in the way your parents tell them? Who are those people in the old photo albums? What are the memories that go along with clothes, memorabilia, a sense of time or place, even smells? Their stories can help you build a renewed level of trust that will prove exceptionally valuable when you try to move on to more emotion-laden issues and decisions.

To jog their mental and emotional storytelling files, media can be a great stimulus. Books and magazines, movies and television shows, especially music can call up strong images of days gone by. Visit a

Read More About It

A wonderful reference for your library is *The Oxford Book of Aging*, edited by Thomas R. Cole and Mary G. Winkler (1994: Oxford University Press). The book is broken into chapters that help us understand how aging has been perceived in literature through the ages. The goal of this compilation is to encourage people of all ages to view aging as a season of our lives we have yet to fully embrace. Too commonly, the familiar words from Ecclesiastes – "To every thing there is a season, and a time to every purpose under heaven" – carry little weight when we're talking about the later stages of life. We need to change this.

library or cruise the Internet for memorable images and icons. Find an old movie you remember your parents taking you to. Listen to the music that used to play in the background of your childhood – the soundtrack of your parents' generation.

A word about computers: We take them for granted; our parents look on them as strange and mysterious devices. Their fears are wrong – but they may need you to show them the good side of this ubiquitous and increasingly indispensable technology.

I've seen older adults who have never touched a computer transformed when they realize it's a means to reconnect with the outside world, from their children and grandchildren to museums and favorite places out of their past. When they're energized and feel a connection with the "outside," their world grows again. Plus, learning computer logic is a wonderful way to exercise the brain.

As your caregiver role begins to evolve, don't dodge the turbulence of your mutual pasts. Reexamine it. Acknowledge it. But this time with an eye toward closing gaps and respecting viewpoints that once might have been too emotionally tinged. Our childhood years brought protest against some of the basic ideals our parents grew up taking for granted. Now's your chance to re-engage with them – and perhaps smooth some rough edges off family memories.

Revisiting those memories also can take you back to some warm and wonderful times. Recognize that and resolve to make good use of the time you have left with your parents as a family.

CHAPTER 2

Style vs. Substance: Communicating Across The Generational Divide

Communication within families brings with it a lot of emotional baggage. We first learn to communicate from our unique place in a specific family system. Now, as our parents age and we, their adult children, find ourselves called upon to provide increasing amounts of care, support and often initiative, it's not uncommon to run smack into the wall of our past relationships and how they shaped our style of communicating. In this chapter, we'll focus on what that means for us as we take on this new – and unexpected – role of caregiver.

Our families are the first hierarchical institution we experience, the place where we feel most connected – but sometimes also most limited. There's a reason for that: When we were children, our parents had power and control over us. Best case, that created a sense of comfort and closeness. But it most likely did so in the context of clearly differentiated roles.

Now, those roles are different. Not reversed – the image that we're being tasked with "parenting our parents," while sometimes accurate, can just as often skew relationships and aggravate long-buried tensions and insecurities. In the Introduction, Dick Schaaf suggests that for us, the root issue is the same – independence – but with very different flashpoints: taking hold of pieces of our parents' lives rather than systematically letting go of our children's.

Understanding what's in play when we communicate across the generations is a key step in helping our parents – and helping ourselves – adjust to the realities of their aging selves.

Who You Were When

Communication is a crucial life skill, but one most of us haven't had much chance to practice, on an adult level, within our family systems. Time and time again, I've found myself working with anguished adult children of seniors who are fully capable, even eloquent, in communicating at work and as parents to their own children, yet totally tongue-tied, and even intimidated, when it comes to talking with mom and dad about things that matter.

It's nobody's fault, though it's natural to want to blame someone for what can be a painfully dissatisfying situation. Before you get frustrated with yourself, or your parents, think back. What kind of communication did you have with your parents when you were growing up? Was it open and frank? Was it based on ignoring unpleasant realities? Was purposeful conversation a normal occurrence in everyday family life? Or a sign that something was wrong and required "correction"? Importantly, did the balance of power shift toward a relationship of equals as you grew up, or did the top-down model persist – perhaps eventually pushing you away because your parents simply weren't good at letting go?

There is a bittersweet balance in this power and control dance, and it affects communication in all kinds of ways, from the words you choose – and hear – to the silent forms of body language and facial expression you've learned to recognize through the years. My Mom was an alcoholic: She didn't even have to talk sometimes to communicate her mood to us.

The way we communicate as adults today has its roots in how we once interacted with our parents way back when. Most of us solidified our self-esteem, or how we experience ourselves, by age 7. If we had low self-esteem then, our communication tends to reflect that now: in not asserting our needs or desires, not asking for what we want, not putting ourselves "out there" where we can be hurt.

On the other hand, those of us who grew up with high self-esteem can come across as very confident and assertive today, fully willing to take hold of whatever we have to, regardless of how it bruises or stings. After all, it's "for their own good." To your parents, that can feel insensitive.

Surprise! Communication doesn't magically become better with time, especially if you haven't had much reason to practice with each other. If you've had issues before, you can expect them to return, even increase, as your parents age – especially if physical, emotional or cognitive issues are becoming of greater concern for them.

Finding New Balance

Think about it from their perspective: Your parents probably aren't used to, let alone comfortable with, coming to you – their child – for help. To them, letting go of important (or even minor) parts of their lives can seem like a sign of weakness, or an admission of failure or decline. And it's not only your communication style that's at issue: If they haven't learned good habits up to now, the way they ask for help will come out anywhere from awkward to, well, horrible.

- They may use shame to get what they want: "I thought you were different from other kids, but I guess you're not."

- Or they'll throw up comparisons you have no way to counter: "Well, so-and-so's kid comes by every day."

- Or they'll make a point of suffering in silence: "Oh, that's okay. You have so much to do already. I don't want to be a bother."

Most of us listen "autobiographically" – we relate everything we hear to our own world. Try tuning in from your parent's side and listen "empathetically" instead. What sounds like control may not be.

Maybe they say, "Hey, I'd like to go to the store with you. Can you wait for me? I'll only take a half-hour and I'll be ready." They may think they're saying they want to do things your way. But from a child's one-down perspective, it sounds like they're exercising control over when you leave, just like when you were a kid.

Words take more meaning from context than from the dictionary. However your childhood experiences positioned you within your family, they have affected your communication style. If they're left unaddressed, they are going to become issues again.

Granting that it can be difficult, try to block out the emotional noise and listen for what's really involved. Your parents need your help. They need the care they're counting on you to give. They just don't know how to ask, or aren't very good at asking gracefully. What's more, they may not be sure you'll respond favorably, or at all (which may say more about *their* self-esteem as parents than anything you have control over).

Don't get caught up in their stuff, though. It's not your loneliness or frustration that's speaking. It's theirs. Sometimes, what they really need is just the opportunity to spout off – to someone whose affection they shouldn't have to doubt, but very well may.

Finding The Real Issues

A friend once asked me, "How do I tell my dad he smells?" I asked him if he would want a friend to tell him if he was the one who smelled. "Yes," he answered. Then tell him like a friend, I suggested: "Hey dad, you have a strong odor. I know I'm not always aware when I smell bad. Just thought I'd tell you." Then let dad respond.

Be prepared, though: Sometimes, you'll have to get well below the tip of the iceberg. Maybe the reason dad smells has nothing to do with hygiene habits. As people age, their sense of smell is one of the first to decline – could be he's not aware. On the other hand, maybe the shower's in the basement, or upstairs, and dad's not real comfortable going up and down stairs these days. Or his balance is a little less steady than he's been letting on. Time to get some grab rails installed, or start looking into one-level living.

Your parents may shut you out when you bring up issues like these. If that happens, you have to let it go. You've said what you needed to say, but our parents get to make their own choices, even if we don't agree with them. You can remind them that you are uncomfortable being around them when they have a strong odor, but don't let it become a wedge that drives you apart.

My tailor dropped off some clothes one day, and I could tell she was frustrated. She had her mom in the car. "She's driving me crazy, always asking when she can go home," she complained. If your parents are in a new or different place – a care community, a nursing home, recovering in the hospital – and they continually ask, "When can I go home," they are most likely pushing *your* emotional buttons because *they* feel powerless to do anything else.

Try to be a researcher: Ask, "What is it about home you miss?" Let them tell you what home means to them and you may get a better understanding of what they are feeling, which can make it easier to respond in an effective way.

It's very human to react irrationally when confronted by realities we don't like but feel powerless to change. My tailor had told her mother that she needed to listen to the doctor when he said she required 24-hour care at home. Unfortunately, all her mom heard was "at home." With childlike simplicity, she was asking her daughter, "When can you come home with me?"

Dodging the unpleasant answer doesn't solve anything. The correct reply is, "I can't. But let me help you find a place where the care – and the caring – will provide what you need."

Confronting Stereotypes

Because of our generally negative views of aging, we can easily treat our parents as if they don't understand us, or are too needy, or are demanding too much of us. That's one more reason it's important to maintain the basic elements of good communication.

For example, I've seen the preoccupied adult child of a senior parent walk into mom's room, pick up some dirty clothes, and turn away saying, "I'll be right back to help you shower" – without ever making eye contact. When she comes back, she's upset to find mom didn't "hear" what she said.

It's not because mom's hard of hearing. Rather, her daughter was so wrapped up in the task at hand that she didn't extend the courtesy of looking at the person to whom she was speaking. She made mom feel like just another burden to be taken care of, one more lump of dirty laundry, rather than an adult who's had a full life, raised kids, and lived independently in the world for decades.

When you need to connect more effectively as a caregiver across the great generational divide, spend at least a little time reevaluating your game:

☺ *Believability* is the key ingredient in effective communication, so be yourself. Talk about what you know. Admit it when you don't know. And don't hide unpleasant or uncomfortable things, the way you would with a child. Remember that far beyond the words you use, vocal (tone of voice) and visual (body language) clues make up 93 percent of your communication effectiveness. Odds are, they'll know you're not saying something. And that may worry them even more.

◉ *Knowing your audience* also is crucial. Communicate with mom and dad based on your understanding of who they are and where they're coming from as adults. Don't speak above or below them. Instead, think of it as playing catch. When you throw a ball to another person, you naturally take into account their ability to catch it. Establish eye contact, throw the ball to their ability, and follow through.

◉ *Listen with your eyes* by looking at the person with whom you're interacting. Isn't it irritating when you're trying to carry on a conversation and the other person is constantly looking around? When you're in a conversation, be with that person, nowhere else. Tune out your own worries and other distractions and be present in the moment. It may help to tune out other disrupters, too: Turn off the TV, don't answer the phone, and put your multi-tasking home and business personality into one-track mode for awhile.

◉ *Stay on message* by focusing on what your parents need from you. When emotional buttons are pushed, we tend to get defensive. Knowing that, keep the protective covers in place. Your parents' emotions are theirs. It's their anger, their sadness, their frustration. Breathe, then say to yourself, "This is their stuff." Practice and it will improve.

Communication is a skill developed over time. It's not something that comes naturally. And just as high self-esteem leads to good communication, good communication is a reflection of high self-esteem. When you take on a caregiver role with your parents, the slate's not blank. Decades of emotional baggage, good and bad, happy and sad, are already there, just waiting for you.

That said, anyone, at any age, can work to improve the way they communicate. Don't accept the comfortable excuses: "That's just who I am." "I'm too old to change." "Too much water has gone over that dam."

We're never too old. Too stuck, maybe – but never too old. And if ever you needed to find a reason for change, what could be better than helping your parents as they discover how much they need you in their lives?

CHAPTER 3

Through Different Eyes: Children's Books And Aging

End-of-life issues are complex all by themselves. Multiply them by different personalities, all the cumulative worries being carried around by all of you, and perhaps decades of avoiding substantive challenges, and you'll find a pretty huge elephant camped in your living room.

Here's an uncommon way to reduce it to a manageable size: As many of us learn in our own parenting, when you need to deal with a delicate issue in a positive, non-threatening way, children's books can get to the heart of the matter quickly, simply and with great warmth. Aging and end-of-life issues are no exception.

Check your stereotypes at the door, though: There's nothing "childish" in connecting through these rich resources. In fact, there can be a degree of psychological comfort for adult children and aging parents alike, especially if mom or dad read to you in your earliest years.

The fact is children's books can provide a simple, safe vehicle through which family members of many ages can come to grips with the ultimate realities of aging. After all, more players may be involved here than just you and your parents. Your children and grandchildren see your parents aging, too. In the welcoming pages of a children's book, you may find new ways to open long-delayed conversations and strengthen lines of family communication.

Consider Shel Silverstein's wondrous *The Giving Tree* (1964: HarperCollins). Is it positive or negative? Is it happy or sad? To me, its beauty is in its ambiguity: Few books offer so much meaning without telling you what they intend to mean. I've often thought it would be an interesting challenge to rewrite the ending. Try it with your parents and see what you think.

Here are four more children's books that engage the issues of aging in anything but childish ways.

Spirituality In Old Age:
Old Turtle, by Douglas Wood; watercolors by Cheng-Khee Chee (1992: Scholastic Books).

In 1990, Eric's Mom announced that she wanted to start collecting children's books. The first book I gave her was *Old Turtle*. As an inscription, I wrote: "May you find peace when you read this book. May you find God, too."

At any point in our lives, we may wonder who God is, or search for a way to describe God, especially to someone younger. My nephew Davin asked about God at a very young age. When I read him *Old Turtle*, it helped him begin to formulate some ideas. As they confront their own mortality, your parents may find themselves on the same path as young children, but at different places. For them (and you), this book can be equally powerful.

Old Turtle is the book's god figure. She's the one who tells all the different animals and birds and plants in nature to stop squabbling over who's most important: Every kind has a place. When people arrive, she gives them the same timeless message: Stop fighting. Everything in nature is there for a reason. It's all important.

This is a splendid book to read aloud – and a good one for your parents to read to their grandchildren and great-grandchildren. Because it deals (however nondenominationally) with the idea of God, it may offend some people. But it speaks so much about beauty and love that I find it hard to believe you won't find some parts that speak directly to you, too.

Don't stop after you read the book once through. By working – separately or together – to pick out music to accompany the different parts, you can deepen the book's meaning and broaden its value. There are two quiet parts and two angry parts. Each time I've been involved in finding music for them, my experience of the book has changed. The act of choosing the music helps the story evolve and come alive.

 Picking music to accompany words can be a daunting task, so

make sure everyone takes the time to read the book first. Classical, rock, spiritual, it doesn't matter. What matters is how the music helps your family tell – and experience – the story in its own special way.

Passing On Values:
Miss Rumphius, by Barbara Cooney (1985: Puffin).

Children's stories about aging or older adults haven't always painted a positive picture of growing older. Barbara Cooney's *Miss Rumphius*, a winner of the American Book Award, puts a positive spin on the wisdom of older adults.

It's a wonderful story illustrating the need to not only live a full life, but also to give something back to the world. Little Alice learns this lesson on her grandpa's lap and grows into Miss Rumphius, who becomes known as the "Lupine Lady" because of the beauty she leaves behind in the form of lupines.

(Quick test of your frame of reference: If you have some gardeners in the family, you may know the lupine – sometimes spelled lupin – as a flower popularly called the bluebonnet. If you have some Monty Python fans, you may flash on the classic sketch where a cockeyed bandit steals lupines from the rich and gives them to the poor – only to learn they'd much rather have food. Or gold.)

Miss Rumphius takes her cue from her grandfather, who encouraged her to travel and experience different cultures, but also told her she needed to do something to make the world more beautiful. Now she's very old, and her niece and groups of children gather around her to hear stories from her life's adventures, giving her the chance to pass on her own lesson of living well and finding some way to beautify the earth. There are some stereotypes – little old lady with white hair, for starters – but overall, age and aging are treated with tenderness and honor.

To make this story unique to your family, ask your parents what life lessons they want to pass on to their grandchildren, nieces and nephews. We learn valuable lessons from our elders. When these lessons are told in the form of stories, we remember them even more vividly and lastingly (more about this in Chapter 14).

At the same time, ask yourself what your family is doing to make the world more beautiful. If you can't come up with a satisfying answer, this might be the time for some multi-generational brainstorming to find your family's equivalent of lupines – a legacy you'd like to leave.

Don't just talk about it. Follow the brainstorming with activities. It could be as simple as getting the family together to paint a park bench, or sweep a sidewalk, or pick up litter. Whatever you come up with, involve multiple generations – in particular, your parents, who may find great pride in serving as the inspiration for this kind of family time.

I will never forget walking with my Grandma Jo. Besides taking me on very long walks (and occasionally "getting lost" – a fun way to tire out a tireless child), she always carried a bag with her so she could collect trash along the way. Just as that left an impression on me, seeing your parents' values in action will give their children, and grandchildren, and great-grandchildren something to remember them by long after they're gone.

How To Avoid Loneliness:
The Old Woman Who Named Things, by Cynthia Rylant; illustrated by Kathryn Brown (1996: Harcourt Brace).

"Old people are lonely" is one of the most common myths about aging, and often a tough issue to engage. It is true that some older adults are lonely. But it's also true that some younger adults are lonely, too. So is the old woman in *The Old Woman Who Named Things.* Tired of knowing friends that she can no longer call by name – friends who have died – she decides to name things that she knows she can never outlive.

She names her car. She names her house. She names her bed and favorite chair. But when a little puppy comes to visit, she refuses to give him a name, knowing she may outlive him. The puppy grows into a dog and falls into a routine of visiting the old woman daily. After feeding the dog, she tells him to go away. He does, but always returns the next day.

When he fails to return one day, the old woman worries and goes out looking for him. Mind you, she hasn't given the dog a name, so when she calls the pound and they ask for the dog's name, she has to give him one to claim him. Her fear of becoming too attached is traded in for the joy of knowing him and enjoying him in the present moment.

They may or may not show it, but many of our parents struggle with loneliness at some point. One of the toughest lessons in life is to realize that we will lose people we love along life's way. They know that better than most. But that doesn't mean they should stop meeting new people, or give up their links to old friends.

You can use this book to encourage your parents to reach out and risk calling someone new by name. You also can use it as a catalyst in helping them talk about things that have personal meaning – including the people they're especially afraid of losing. Like family.

Talking about loneliness is the first step to addressing it. *The Old Woman Who Named Things* can help start the conversation.

Talking About Death:
Annie and the Old One, by Miska Miles; illustrated by Peter Parnall (1971: Little, Brown).

The most difficult topic for many families to address is death itself. In our society, it's common to avoid talking of death altogether. Though our media is chock full of mayhem, that stuff happens to strangers. On a personal level, death is uncomfortable, unpleasant and sad.

Death also is natural. Miska Miles presents the concept to children beautifully in her book *Annie and the Old One*. Its elegantly simple approach may help you engage the subject with your parents.

A young Navajo girl and her grandmother are best friends. They walk, talk, laugh and work together. It is fall, and grandmother announces that when the new rug is taken off the loom, she will "return to Mother Earth."

Annie clearly understands this as death, but that doesn't mean she accepts it. To buy more time with her beloved grandmother, she attempts to sabotage the finishing of the rug. She misbehaves at school, reasoning that if her parents have to come talk with her teacher, it will stop the weaving for a day. She lets the sheep out, causing her parents to spend a day searching and then herding them back home. Annie even goes so far as to pull out yarn from the rug.

These small attempts don't accomplish her goal of keeping grand-mother from dying. They can't. But from her grandmother, Annie learns that there is a natural order to things, and it's futile to work against that. Death simply is part of life.

Using *Annie and the Old One*, you might compare notes with your parents on things you've tried, tricks you've played, to make something last longer. Anyone ever "get lost" on vacation to avoid having to return home? From that, connect the dots: What arcane little habits and superstitions do members of the family use to avoid talking about or dealing with difficult issues? In particular, death.

Reading children's books together can provide a comforting, heart-warming and engaging way to connect the generations. They also serve to remind us that lessons simply written can be very powerful and life-affirming.

Consider these five books, but know that there are countless more available to you, many reflecting specific cultures, religions, time-frames and personal beliefs. A few hours on the Internet can point you at dozens of possibilities. So can a good research librarian at your local library – a seriously underutilized resource in most communi-ties. Ask. You'll be amazed.

But don't "own" this all by yourself. Involve your siblings, your children – and especially your parents – in the quest for new ways to see old age through the youngest of eyes.

Mental, Emotional and Physical Health

In 1900, the average life expectancy in the United States was 47. Today, most members of the Baby Boom Generation have long since surpassed that mark, and the rest of us are in sight of it.

If that puts us on uncharted ground, imagine what it has done to our parents – perhaps the longest-lived generation ever. They're living longer, more active and generally more satisfying lives than those who have gone before them. But nothing lasts forever.

As a caregiver, you can find yourself coping with any number of new and often frightening threats to their health: mental, emotional and physical. When the situation becomes dire or difficult, you'll have to rely on the skills of specialists. The longer you can help your parents hold off such situations, the more time you and they will have to enjoy together.

In the chapters that follow, I'll show you that mental decline is not an inevitable part of aging. I'll try to convince you of the importance of playing, even as you devote time to your parents as a caregiver – for your own mental and emotional health as much as for your parents'. And I'll give you some simple "steps" you can take – literally – to help your parents stay physically active and fit (which will do wonders for their mental health and emotional outlook, too).

43 Measuring Up

With paper and pencil at hand, draw the following WITHOUT MEASURING:

~ A line two inches long

~ A line the length of an average common straight pin

~ A line the length of a new standard pencil

~ A rectangle the size of a standard playing card

~ A circle the size of a penny

~ A circle the size of a quarter

~ A line the length of your foot

~ A rectangle the size of a regular postage stamp

~ A circle the size of an electrical outlet

Now compare your drawings with the actual objects to see how accurate your perceptions are.

CHAPTER 4

Taking Care Of The Mind: Mental Health And Brain Aerobics

It's not true, but most Americans believe it: Getting old means our cognitive abilities decline. Forever. For your parents, this may well be their single greatest fear as they age. Contrary to the enduring myths, however, loss of intellect, memory and creative problem-solving doesn't happen suddenly (or slowly, for that matter) just because we "get old." In fact, it isn't a necessary part of aging at all.

Pop quiz: Consider these six statements – true or false?

⊚ Between age 40 and 50, you can expect your mental powers to begin to decline.

⊚ Memory loss is a natural part of the aging process.

⊚ Once memory "goes," nothing can bring it back.

⊚ There is nothing you can do to slow the aging of your brain.

⊚ Chronic confusion and forgetfulness are the first symptoms of approaching dementia.

⊚ Older people cannot develop creative ability.

How'd you do? All six true? Four out of six? Two out of six?

Try none out of six! The brain is like a muscle. The more it's exercised and used, the healthier and more resilient it becomes. In and of itself, aging doesn't change this. More often than not, the mental symptoms we commonly associate with advancing age can be traced to other causes. A vitamin, mineral or dietary deficiency. Lack of stimulation and use. Depression. Sometimes, medication can create confusion and forgetfulness. So can booze. A decline in the body's overall health and well-being can affect the brain.

Consequently, loss of memory and mental function are not inevitable. If you're willing to help your parents work at it, they can actually improve both. Similarly, studies show that creative abilities can be developed at any age.

Neurons And Dendrites?

Don't confuse the mind with the brain. The mind is "software," the mystical and mysterious product of all that we are. The brain is "hardware," a bodily organ that requires nutrition, rest, regular use, and proper medical care. Because the brain is flesh and blood, we need to take the same interest in its overall health as we do with the other organs in our bodies.

The key players in brain function are neurons (brain cells) and their dendrites. As a simplistic analogy, think of neurons like tiny tree trunks. Dendrites are the branches. Our brains have 100 billion neurons, give or take a few – as many as the Milky Way has stars. When the brain is active, the dendrites on a neuron reach out and electrical signals leap across to link them to other dendrites on other neurons. According to Marge Engelman in *Aerobics of the Mind* (1996: Attainment Company), "Researchers estimate that the normal brain has a quadrillion connections between the brain cells, more than all the phone calls made in the United States in the past decade."

The more brain activity, the more connections, and the more our brains (as seen through wondrous tools like MRIs) look like dense thickets. When the brain doesn't stay active, or is affected by diseases and alien substances (including alcohol), the neurons die, dendrites shrink, and the once thick forest looks like a sparse woods.

The point: You want to do everything you can to make sure the brain resembles a thick forest. That way, according to Paul David Nussbaum, Ph.D., a clinical neuropsychologist who specializes in brain health and aging across the lifespan, if "the weed-whacker of dementia comes through, there's a lot more to cut down."

Thinking Healthy

There are four essential goals in helping your parents stay mentally sharp:

1. Preventing brain degeneration.

2. Optimizing brain function.

3. Improving cognitive function, especially in persons with mild cognitive impairment (which healthcare professionals like to abbreviate MCI).

4. Slowing the progression of dementias, such as Alzheimer's.

For most people, 20 percent of brain cells die over the course of a lifetime. But since we have billions, natural attrition is not the culprit in the mental myths of aging. Without brain-stimulating exercise, on the other hand, the dendrites become scrawny rather than lush, which is why function and capacity often diminish in seniors.

To prevent this, you need to help your parents preserve or develop habits that keep their brains active, ideally on a daily basis. Here are three tactical ways to do that.

Storytelling And Reminiscence

Most of us know that our parents enjoy going back in time. What we may fail to understand is how important telling their own stories can be for them in the present. Our parents can sometimes get lost in their own world, cut off from family and friends, wallowing in feeling useless. When they're fed up with, don't understand, or feel left out of present-day society, telling their life stories in their own voice allows them to express personal meaning. Giving them the chance to tell those stories again (or perhaps for the very first time) can help them reconnect with life – and with their children, the part of life with which they may most want to stay connected.

Especially in old age, our parents look to find self-worth in their pasts. Research shows that when people can create a self-narrative from their past, putting life events into a coherent and selective story, the result can be both satisfying and self-justifying. What they accomplished *then* can reinforce self-worth *now*. Plus, the more complete the story is, the more they learn about themselves – and, if we're still listening, the more we learn about them.

Even better, using data from past memory to construct a whole story stimulates the brain in a number of related ways. The exercise of remembering enhances the ability to perform other activities. Past experiences re-enter consciousness and provide data for other mental operations. And the refreshed memories stay vivid for the next time they're accessed.

Brain Workouts

Doing "aerobics of the mind" is another way to preserve and enhance mental health. Exercising the brain is as important as exercising the body. Just as your parents' physical health will surely decline if they spend all day stuck in a chair, with no activity to stimulate their bodies, giving the brain nothing to do will contribute to progressive mental decline as well.

The idea of brain aerobics is to incorporate neuron-stimulating exercises into the daily routine to help your parents stay mentally fit. (These exercises also will help reduce stress, by the way.) There are a growing number of systematic ways to exercise the brain. The one I'm partial to is described in *Aerobics of the Mind* and its associated deck of Mental Fitness Cards, both available from Attainment Company, Inc., of Verona, Wisconsin (the publisher of this book – visit www.AttainmentCompany.com or call 800/327-4269).

I first heard about aerobics of the mind at the University of Wisconsin, where Marge Engelman was one of my adult education professors. She had done research on creativity and aging, testing the validity of such enduring myths as "you can't teach an old dog new tricks" on a group of women between the ages of 70 and 90. The results exceeded even her ambitious hypotheses. That led to her book, and later the card deck of brain exercises.

Each card describes a complete, short exercise that can be done solo, or together. Many focus on heightening awareness of specific senses, or changing static behaviors. Others offer pencil-and-paper activities designed to stimulate the memory, creativity or mental acuity. An example of one of the card deck's 100 exercises is reproduced at the beginning of this chapter.

So many of us find it difficult to visit our moms and dads. With nothing else to do, they seem to focus our time and their energy on pushing emotional buttons. Using Marge's Mental Fitness Cards, you can maintain control of your visits and help your parents exercise their brains at the same time.

My friend Lee used to come home from visiting her mom depressed. All she'd hear was, "Why don't you visit more often?" or, "What's wrong with your sister?" I suggested she use mental aerobics as a way to focus her mother on something new and different. The cards gave them both something to do – and something to laugh about. Now, when it's time to go, it's not uncommon for her to hear, "Couldn't we work through one more card?"

Learn Something

Using learning to exercise the brain helps build interest in all kinds of things. It also helps enhance (or rebuild) self-esteem in your parents, regardless of their chronological age, while nurturing a sense that not only *can* they learn, but there's still so much *more* to learn. An older man once told me, "I hope I never know everything."

You can help your parents develop stimulating activities around any number of enjoyable pastimes, many of which have a learning component: Doing crossword puzzles, picture puzzles, Sudoku and trivia. Participating in reading groups that pick and discuss books. Learning a language or enrolling in a class. Taking up art or a craft – working with clay, watercolors, quilting. Joining a card club – bridge, rummy, pinochle, poker, whatever (math is a terrific mental energizer). Patronizing the arts, from symphonies to community theater.

You also can make up all kinds of variations on your own. Ever try to count to 100 by threes? Recite the alphabet backwards? Add up the total of the digits in your phone number? Sit two places to the left of your normal seat at a family gathering? Your parents probably haven't, either.

Ruts may be comfortable, but they're not very stimulating to our brains. When we try something new, whether it's counting in a different way, setting the table differently, driving home via a new route, or exploring someplace new, we are encouraging our brains to think in a non-habitual way. That kind of exercise pays all kinds of dividends.

Here are five learning games to try with your parents, drawn from Marge Engelman's work, my own, and Cynthia S. Short's *Grow Dendrites Forever: 1998 Brain Fitness Kit* (1997: Cynorge).

Use your senses: Using only the sense noted: (a) go to a bakery and make a purchase by smell alone; (b) go to a florist and enjoy the variety of flowers by smell alone; (c) go to a fabric store and enjoy the variety of materials by touch alone; (d) go to the fruit section of your grocery store and enjoy the variety by color alone.

Measuring up: With paper and pencil at hand, take turns drawing the following without measuring: (a) a line two inches long; (b) a line the length of an average common straight pin; (c) a line the length of a standard pencil; (d) a circle the size of a quarter; (e) the shape of the state where you live.

Tap the inner poet: My brother, Steven Augustus, is a poet. Much of his poetry I don't fully understand, but he reminds me to let it speak to me. Just to me. There isn't one and only one meaning within a poem. It's up to the reader to uncover its personal meaning. Whether your parents have found meaning in poetry throughout their lives, or are coming to it fresh – and whether they're writing it or simply reading it – poetry can speak to each of them on an individual level. If you need help understanding poetry, try any of Roger Housden's 10 Poems series.

Seek specific knowledge: Take them to the library (or out onto the Internet) to do some "tasty" research: foods that stimulate the brain, the best times and ways to eat specific foods for optimal benefit, minerals and vitamins that are brain-friendly, herbs that are good for the brain, and so forth. You'll help them use their brain to keep their body healthy while also reminding them to eat regularly and properly.

Think gratitude: Have your parents begin a "gratitude journal" by writing down five things each day that they're grateful for. Then use the journal to help them say thanks. Why five things a day? Because when we're talking upbeat and positive, the more the merrier. You might even encourage them to celebrate by giving small gifts to the people in their lives who do the "little things" so well for them: hairdressers, postal clerks, mail carriers, garbage collectors, the receptionist at the doctor's or dentist's.

The Big Ugly

All this presupposes their brains are still working properly. In recent years, we've become painfully aware that as age increases, so too does the potential for the onset of dementia. It's a scary prospect, but maybe not as scary as we've made it.

Although Alzheimer's and dementia are often used interchangeably, they shouldn't be. The Big Ugly of dementia is an umbrella that has a number of smaller uglies strung under it. A little more than half of all dementias are Alzheimer's. There are a number of other forms, including diseases that have dementia components, such as Huntington's, Parkinson's, Lewy body, vascular dementia and strokes. About 90 percent of all dementias are irreversible, but a few — such as some depressions and so-called "hospital dementia" — can be reversed.

The Alzheimer's Association (www.alz.org) defines dementia as "a general term for loss of memory and other intellectual abilities serious enough to interfere with daily life." We're just beginning to scratch the surface on what "old-timer's disease" really is, but it's safe to say it has quickly become one of the most feared prospects of aging. Some of those fears are overblown. A 2006 study in Australia estimated that only one percent of those aged 60 to 65 suffer from dementia. Between 75 and 79, the incidence was just six percent — 45 percent for those 95 or older.

If you're caregiving for a parent with dementia, here are four ways to cope.

1. Get into their reality. A rapid-onset, non-Alzheimer's dementia took Dick's mom a number of years ago. In time, she hit a "plateau" and stopped regressing noticeably. It makes for disorienting visits. Dick has had long, fluid conversations with her — about absolutely nothing, but which he suspects would sound very normal to someone who didn't know her condition. On one occasion, as they drove down a street, his mom started reading off billboards and street signs with complete accuracy. But when asked to read something specific, she couldn't. In her dementia, the brain was still functioning, but not all of the connections were working as they once did.

While working in Denver, I often found myself "waiting for the bus" with a resident, who, in her mind, was always needing to leave to take care of her children. Of course, there was no bus and her children were all fully grown, but that didn't matter. I waited with her and asked her to tell me more about her kids. That was her reality, and in it she could function with at least the appearance of normalcy.

2. Know their current age. As many dementias progress, memories regress. Families often are upset when they come to visit and find mom isn't wearing her glasses anymore. "She always wore glasses," they protest. Maybe not. In her mind, she's much younger now, and maybe at the age she is, she didn't wear glasses. That's why, if you show her a current picture of herself, she'll probably identify it as her mother or an aunt – and why my Denver resident was focused on getting home to take care of her kids.

Some aspects of dementia are predictable, others aren't. When her dementia came on, Dick's mom "forgot" that she smoked – a couple of packs a day, in fact! Strangely enough, she didn't go through any noticeable physical withdrawal symptoms. Her California memories faded rapidly, but her Ohio memories stayed vivid (the family moved to the West Coast in the '60s). Gradually, she has lost them as well, regressing through the '50s and the '40s to – based on the names she occasionally still brings up – the '30s. (She was born in 1923.)

3. Don't argue, guide. People with dementia can be stubborn – and the more you try to push them to do something, the harder they'll resist. Speak to them simply. Pause to let things sink in. Don't hurry them, or scold them, let alone try to "reason" with them. They're not likely to make the connections that seem so clear and obvious to you.

I remember how hard it sometimes was to get someone with Alzheimer's to shower. "I don't want to shower," they'd say with maddening simplicity. "But you have to," family members would argue, generally managing only to further frustrate themselves. Better to say, "I don't like to either, but tomorrow is Sunday and you told me we had to be clean for church." Diversion works for some. With others, if you know the age they're currently at and something about the conditions in which they grew up, you can try to link to memories from an earlier time. Maybe they didn't shower when they were younger, but the prospect of a bath meets no resistance at all.

4. Turn off the TV. People with dementia often have trouble processing, or even understanding, things they see on television. The images look very real, but happen so much faster. In too many care facilities, I see the TV used as an electronic babysitter, with no thought to what people with dementia are seeing. I've seen a resident in a memory-care home get up and go look behind the TV to find out where people are hiding.

Often, what they're seeing on TV shows are situations they think they must solve. If a character asks another for money, they worry about where to send a check. My Grandpa Gus once was convinced that he had to go to San Francisco right away. Why? They needed him to solve a rape, he told us.

An exception to the rule are movies, especially familiar ones with no commercials. Some of my residents in Denver knew all of the words to the songs in *The Sound of Music*, and singing while they watched provided a clear sense of comfort.

I don't, by any means, aspire to become TV's "Kari Nation," but I can't help but suggest that your parents will find they have a lot more time for brain-engaging activities if they recognize one of the greatest threats to their mental fitness. It's sitting right in front of them – or, more accurately, they're sitting in front of it, perhaps for far too many hours a day: the television set.

Yes, TV opens a window on the world. But it's a passive window. We observe, typically in isolation. We don't interact. We don't connect. We don't engage in the mental ping-pong game of conversation.

There's a reason they call it "the boob tube."

CHAPTER 5

At Any Age, In Any Place: Playing Is Good For You

In Chapter 4, we dealt with some tough stuff. So let's play for a while!

Shortly after my Mom died in 2002, Dad, my sister Anne and I decided we'd watch the Academy Awards and dress as if we were attending. Even though it was soon after my mother's death, playing "dress up" helped all of us have a silly, wonderful time. It didn't lessen our grief. But it did help us keep it from consuming us.

Helping your parents deal with the issues of aging – physical, mental, emotional, financial, geographical – will test your balance and stamina. It will stress your spouse, your family, your work life, your basic sense of self. Sometimes, it will bring you a level of joy that will surprise you. Sometimes, it will bring you down.

No matter how serious things get, you owe it to yourself, and everyone who loves you, to preserve a sense of fun. It may seem simple advice to give, but odds are you'll find it difficult to do as the responsibilities – and sheer amount of time – involved in caregiving begin to mount up.

No matter how tough it gets, remember: Life goes on. It goes on better with a smile.

Childlike, Not Childish

Unfortunately, in our society, playing is often considered a mindless activity, one usually permitted to children, but not to adults. Sure, you can play when you're playing with children. But to play on your own or with other adults is generally frowned upon, especially if you have other, supposedly more "serious" or "important" things to do. By one estimate, before we send them off to school, our children laugh about 300 times a day. The average for adults? Just 17 times a day. Uff-da!

If you're not connected to kids on a daily basis, it's sometimes difficult to give yourself permission to play. "Act your age," is what we're told. Forget that noise – act your smarts instead! By now, you should have learned how important it is to leaven the tough stuff with some laughter. All you're doing when you let an overactive sense of dignity and decorum dictate your actions and attitudes is setting yourself up for a big fall. And that brings us back full circle, because when you're the caregiver, your parents are depending on you not to fall.

Much of playing has to do with letting go. Let go of what others will think. Let go of the negative self-talk or your fears of appearing silly. Often, silly is the point of the exercise. That voice in your head saying, "I don't have time for this kind of foolishness," or "It's too late to try something new," is really just fear of embarrassment talking.

If you are someone who dares to try new things, who can and does play like no one is watching, you'll find you have a better attitude and more energy for your caregiving activities, as well as for your family and the "rest of your life." Plus, you'll be a positive influence on your parents whenever they're feeling that there's no fun left in life. Live light-hearted and know that play is good for the heart, soul and brain – yours and theirs.

Back To Basics

As far as I can tell, there is no rulebook for how to act in our later years. The first step is to forget what society says – or what we think society says. Playing, goofing around, being silly, finding fun even in serious issues are all good for the soul. That, in turn, is good for our parents. They face enough serious issues in their later years. The last thing they need is kids whose periodic visits take on the feeling of daylong drizzles.

When we play, we allow our creativity to bloom. The more we can tap into what it was like to be a child, without reservation, willing to try and fail, even make a fool of ourselves on occasion, the freer we are to play. The key distinction is to play in a childlike manner, rather than a childish one.

Whenever I feel stuck, bored, frustrated, I know it's time to play. Here are some "play basics" to reorient you to your sense of fun, no matter what else may be going on in your parents' lives. Or yours.

Accentuate the positive: Before you can play, you need to get the negative messages about play out in the open. You'll hear people (maybe yourself!) say things like, "We are adults; play is for children." Say what? At what age did you stop playing? Why?

At any age, play is a good thing. It stimulates and refreshes the mind and body alike. Don't let life, work, people and events around you, or the weight of the adult responsibilities you carry, interfere with your willingness or your ability to lighten up and have a little fun from time to time.

In working with seniors, I often introduce the idea of playing by having them write down the negative messages they've heard about it throughout their lives. Try it, both by yourself and with your parents. Then crumple up the excuses and make a positive commitment to play.

Define play: What does play look like when you "get it right?" Play can be anything from a casual (or cutthroat) game of cards to walking barefoot in the grass. It's also being silly, laughing at jokes, having a picnic in the moonlight, going to a ten-tissue movie. The important thing to remember is that it's play, not work: Let go of the idea that you absolutely have to do things right or perfect. When we play, it's okay to mess up, to not get it right. Play is not outcome-based – there is no right way to color. The fun is in the doing.

I had to learn that lesson literally. A few years ago, I was working on a wonderfully involved project, but it had come to a standstill. I didn't know where to go next. Needing a break, I asked my husband if he would lie on the floor and color with me. He took the left side and I did the right. At one point, I stopped and looked at his side. "You're coloring so much better than I am," I remember saying. He laughed and said, "This isn't a competition. It's just coloring."

D'oh! Just coloring. Let go, Grasshopper, let go. Play is just about doing something, not about judging what you're doing. Play is about letting go. And that's where some of us – myself obviously included – get into trouble. We haven't learned to just let ourselves go play. It doesn't feel safe, or like it's the right thing to do.

In reality, we've learned how not to let ourselves go, at least not the way we did when we were children. When we were kids, we could just play. And did. Sometimes, that's all we did – all day. That's what we need to rediscover: that childlike (not childish) sense of wonder and joy in the simplest of things. Sneak it in, if you have to.

Find time to play: One of the constants on the lists of negative messages my seniors came up with was, "I don't have time for play." Sure you do. You just forgot where to look for it. So look. Read a joke. Tell a joke. Watch a pet do something goofy. Sometimes, my Dad and I just get up and dance – for no reason at all other than we like to. Yes, it's good for our emotional health, but that's not why we do it. It makes us feel good.

If we constantly work, work, work, without relief, our brains – and our bodies – begin failing us. Want an upside? Playing actually helps us get things done. Think about times you've struggled to complete a task, becoming more and more frustrated with yourself. Then someone does something funny, you laugh – and suddenly the task is not so difficult. When we shift our thoughts and do something out of the ordinary, our brains are refreshed and begin humming along again.

Our bodies benefit, too. Helpguide (www.helpguide.org), a website promoting active, healthy lifestyles, offers this quote from the Discovery Channel's Discovery Health website: "When we laugh, natural killer cells which destroy tumours and viruses increase, along with Gamma-interferon (a disease-fighting protein), T-cells (important for our immune system) and B-cells (which make disease-fighting antibodies). As well as lowering blood pressure, laughter increases oxygen in the blood, which also encourages healing."

Worth noting: Structured forms of play take time, and that's a good thing. Whether you're playing cards, or checkers, or Monopoly, or miniature golf, a game provides its own stimulus for conversation and other brain-boosting interactions, and has its own dimension of time. You're not done playing at eight o'clock on the dot. You're done when the game's done.

Time with you is something your parents may crave more than they know. Nothing says you can't spend your time together playing. After all, the time you spend playing with them is *time you spend with them*. If you're constantly checking your watch when you're with your parents, or fidgeting trying to find something else to chatter about while wondering how soon you can beat a hasty retreat, odds are you really need to play.

Old Age: A No-Fun Zone?

We've established that maintaining a sense of fun brightens your day and improves your health. Just imagine what it can do for your parents. When life becomes focused on negatives, when energy is harder to come by, it's difficult to let a sense of play in. Yet, no matter how unwilling they may appear – and is that truly *them*, or a pattern of thinking about them *you've* fallen into? – they need to have fun. Study after study shows that fun is good for our health, while a lack of it contributes to everything from simple illnesses to deep depressions.

For some of our parents, play will be a natural and normal part of the day's routine. For others, it'll be virtually a new habit to develop – or rediscover. Regardless, we need to help them get rid of the barriers that don't allow them to play.

This is a place where connecting to the past may help. What do they recall about playing as a child? About playing with their children? Help them draw a mental picture of what play once looked like and felt like, then assist them in finding ways to experience that feeling again today.

For example, if your mom used to push her kids on the swings, an outing to a local playground just to watch kids swinging could bring a feeling of play back into her life. If she's physically able, sit with her on the swings – your participation reinforces her permission to play. (Careful, though: Many flexible swing seats are hard on older women's hips!)

If you're caring for someone with dementia, remember to laugh with them. They haven't lost their sense of humor. Think coloring is childish? For some seniors, it's a serious form of play: an outlet for creativity, a way to exercise hand-eye coordination, something that requires focus and conceptual thought and sustained activity.

Coloring and other forms of play do have some risks, especially when they demean or diminish, or make our parents uncomfortably conscious of how much they can no longer do. However rare or unanticipated such by-products may be, keep an eye on how your parents are reacting. If they're not having fun, they're going to become more resistant to the idea of playing, not less.

I remember setting up my Mom's medications one day with Anne and my Dad. We were laughing and joking with each other – and all of a sudden, my Mom shouted, "This isn't funny; I need to understand." The fun was helping us cope, but it wasn't helping her, which meant it wasn't the time to be silly.

Be sensitive to your parents' day-to-day realities. Some are probably less independent than they're used to being. Some may be less mobile. For some, their bodies likely are constantly reminding them that there's less they can do. They may be losing connections to friends and family – reading the obituaries in the daily newspaper too often confirms that one more valued (or casual) acquaintance has died. A big outing may involve going to the doctor or dentist. The prospect of a visitor, even if only for a hurried hour or so, may be a rare treat. Otherwise, the high point of their day may center around the mail carrier's arrival. Or the TV.

For them, letting play into their lives may have become progressively more difficult. In some ways, they may even have come to

What Planet Are *You* From?

For a wild look at creativity and play, check out SARK, a woman from Berkeley, California, who has written several books on creativity and has one of the more colorful mental playgrounds on the Web: www.planetsark.com.

Paging through her books is uplifting and playful in and of itself. As she writes in *Eat Mangoes Naked* (2001: Simon & Schuster): "Pleasure and joy invite our best selves out to play and quiet our critical voices."

They are fantastic books to have available and great resources for getting you in the mood to play. But be warned: She handwrites them, they are colorful, and her suggestions are sometimes very wild indeed.

think of it as out of character for them "at this age." If you don't bring a little fun with you, it may be beyond your parents' ability to generate it on their own. But if you can inject a little fun into even ordinary things, for them as well as for you, you'll find it helps offset the bad times when they come.

Brighten Up

Of course, lack of fun is not a universal hallmark of older years by any means. Defying the negatives above, your parents may be the kind who are ever out and about, positively bouncing from one event to another. Whether due to their personalities or the general state of their health (not to mention their finances), their days may have an energy about them that allows new ideas, including letting go and playing.

For them, you need to be more "fun fan" than instigator. Don't second-guess or think it's somehow your job to get them to be serious or settle down. Play along with them – when they want you to. Get out of the way and encourage them when they're obviously getting their fun done on their own.

Caregiving means taking care of some tough issues. Don't let it consume you. Give yourself permission to laugh and include some fun time – schedule it, if you have to. Bring wigs to the hospital. Dress up. Play games. Dance. Sing silly songs.

Play can be vicarious or active, structured or just plain goofy. Either way, it's play.

CHAPTER 6

When Two Left Feet (Or More)
Is A Good Thing:
Walking … And Pets

Regular activity is one of the most important steps your parents can take to maintain their physical and mental health, not to mention their quality of life. The scientific evidence is overwhelming: Being active helps reduce the risk of obesity, high blood pressure, high cholesterol, joint and muscular pain, diabetes, osteoporosis, stroke, depression, colon cancer … and premature death. It increases cardio-vascular (heart and lung) fitness, muscle strength, sends oxygen to the brain, and improves endurance. Yet, based on numerous studies, more than 60 percent of older adults are inactive.

Ironically, your parents face the same basic obstacle to being more physically active as your children do: too much sitting! As an added complication, exercise used to be something their generation got from daily living. Whether it was work on the farm, or at the plant, or housework, or out in the yard, it wasn't something they had to "fit in," let alone manufacture artificially. Now they may need to.

The good news is exercise does not have to be vigorous, or done for a long time, in order to improve your parents' health. And the simplest and most body-friendly form of physical exercise you can recommend to them is simply walking.

The Benefits Of Walking

Walking is low impact, requires minimal equipment, can be done at any time of day, and can be performed at virtually any pace. Yet it's as great a workout for those new to exercise as for those who've spent their lifetimes being physically active. You can get your parents into walking without worrying about many of the risks associated with other, more vigorous forms of exercise: sprains and strains, high cardiovascular stress, the dangers involved in using equipment improperly or too strenuously.

Medically speaking, walking is a "weight bearing" exercise – you carry your own body weight when you walk. It takes very little time to achieve real benefits: Just 30 minutes several times a week, at as brisk a pace as they find comfortable. (Informal definition: "Brisk" means they can talk while walking, but not sing, and may end up puffing slightly.) If they can't walk for 30 minutes at one time, they can achieve the same benefits by walking for 10 minutes three times a day.

To stay on task and turn this into a rewarding long-term habit, it helps a lot to have a buddy – even a group or club – to walk with. This is especially important if one of your parents has died, or is in a care facility separated from their life's partner, and you're trying to help the other one stay active. The little bit of peer pressure a walking buddy provides can help get them out of the chair and into motion. Plus, the social interaction, including before and after the walk, breaks down the walls that can have them feeling isolated, even depressed, as well as inactive.

Tip: When you go to visit your parents, wear your walking shoes and make walking a routine part of your visits.

Walking Smart

Okay, here come the inevitable disclaimers. You should never start an exercise program without first getting a checkup. The same holds true for your parents, the more so if they have physical conditions that need to be taken into account: joint pain, plantar fasciitis and other foot problems, brittle bones, diminished eyesight (including depth perception and peripheral vision), even hearing loss.

The right "equipment" is also crucial – in this case, a good pair of walking shoes. The old riddle asks, what do shoes, beds and tires have in common? Answer: We spend a lot of time using them, but very little time choosing them.

In most cities of any size, there are shoe stores that specialize in fitting older adults, especially those with conditions that affect mobility and balance, including arthritis, diabetes and orthopedic problems. In addition, special inserts (called "orthotics") can be added to counteract a variety of conditions. Make sure your parents get them custom-fitted rather than just buying something hanging on a rack in a store.

Warming up and cooling down are important habits to develop. The best way to "get loose" is to walk slowly, starting off at a leisurely pace to give muscles time to warm up, then picking up speed. They can cool down by gently stretching their leg muscles – particularly their calves and front and back thighs. Stretches should be held for about 20 seconds. If they feel any pain, they should ease off the stretch.

Also, they should avoid bouncing or jolting, which can overstretch muscle tissue and cause microscopic tears. The body continues to burn energy after exercise, so caution them not to cool down too quickly. A gradual cool-down also helps prevent muscle stiffness and injury.

Take A Deep ...

In any exercise program, breathing is always a good place to start. Not only is it good for the body, it's good for the brain. Like our muscles, our brains need oxygen to work at maximum efficiency, so taking time to take a deep breath or two, both when beginning exercise, and during it, helps refuel the body from top to bottom. When we're breathing fully, we think better.

Here's a simple approach – practice it, then work with your parents on it. Sit up straight, arms at your sides. Breathe in through your nose for a count of 4, hold the breath for a count of 7, and exhale through the mouth for a count of 8. Breathe from the abdomen, taking nice, full breaths. Do at least three repetitions. You'll not only think better, you'll feel better.

When exercising, it's best to dress lightly. Dressing too warmly can increase sweating and build up body temperature, which can make them uncomfortable during a walk and possibly cause skin irritations. Dressing lightly lets the body work to raise its own temperature, which burns more energy.

Give some thought to where they'll walk. There's safety in numbers, but there's also safety in paying attention to the surrounding area: If they feel vulnerable, they're less likely to venture out on a regular basis. Take into account potential hazards such as vehicle traffic, uneven or rough surfaces, steep hills, and the influence of wind and weather. Rather than a straight-line path, where the road back can feel intimidatingly long, help them lay out looping routes with multiple opt-outs: shortcuts back to their starting point if they start to feel winded or over-tired.

Cold weather doesn't mean your parents have to hibernate. If they live in the city, nearby shopping centers may have "mall walker" programs designed to encourage fitness without discouraging shoppers. Local health clubs and community centers also may have formal and informal walking programs. In apartment buildings, a few laps up and down the hall can provide a course when the weather's bad. And if there really is no place like home, consider a treadmill or exercise bike – maybe in line of sight of the TV to provide some variety in the "scenery."

Tip: Check their insurance coverage. Some carriers (including some Medicare supplementals, though not Medicare itself, at this writing) recognize the impact on insurance claims of staying active and healthy, and will reimburse, in full or in part, for health-club memberships – provided they're used on a regular basis.

Make sure your parents start their walking program slowly: shorter walks, maybe a couple of times a week until they "get their legs under them," then building from there. It may help them to set specific short-term and long-term goals: a brisk, 10-minute walk (before breakfast, at lunch time, after dinner?) on Monday, Wednesday and Friday, for example, eventually building up to a longer duration most days of the week. For immediate visual reinforcement, hang a calendar in a high-traffic area and have them mark off every day they walk. Make sure you notice it – and compliment them on what it shows – when you visit.

A pedometer (step-counter) is another way to provide immediate feedback and measure progress. It will show them how many steps they take in the course of their day – with or without their walk. Less-active people tend to take about 4,000 steps or fewer per day; 8,000 to 10,000 steps a day is considered the norm for physical fitness. Taking their health into account, they should build toward an achievable target in increments of 250 to 1,000 additional steps of brisk walking. Help them set a realistic goal, then encourage them to log their steps on their fitness calendar. Making progress visible is a proven way to sustain enthusiasm and commitment.

Finally, even if you can't convince your parents to commit to regular exercise, look for ways to encourage them to "sneak in" more walking. Taking the stairs instead of the elevator. Walking to the store or coffee shop instead of driving. Doing their own housework. Walking the neighbors' dog while they're on vacation. Check in with your local community or school district to see if they need "grandparents" to escort young children on their walk to school or serve as crossing guards at busy intersections.

With walking, the possibilities are endless.

Parents And Pets

I am a pet lover – specifically, dogs. Growing up, my German Shepard mix named Heidi was my best friend. I played with Heidi, cried on her furry back and learned about the importance of nature from her. While living in Denver, Eric and I adopted Paddy, an adult Border Collie mix. Paddy was my constant companion as I was growing my business, and often came along when I visited senior living communities. Throughout my life, I've found the company of dogs to be warm and reassuring.

There are numerous good reasons *not* to have an animal as one ages, or so I've been told. I don't buy it. Whether it be a dog, a cat, a bird, a fish, or any other pet, when I hear older adults trying to convince themselves that they don't want or can't have another animal – they live in a condo that doesn't allow pets, or they travel too much to be bothered, or they simply don't want the responsibility, or they don't think they can deal with the prospect of yet another loss – I can't help asking, Why not?

I understand. Pets need attention. Every day. Whether it's cleaning out their litter boxes, or taking them on walks, or filling their food and water bowls, or just making time for them – typically on their schedule, not yours – pets rely on their owners for their daily needs. To me, that's a good thing.

And it might be equally good for your parents. Their home is empty. Their kids are grown, moved out and wrapped up in their own lives. Their friends are becoming fewer or less accessible. Why rule out having someone in their lives who needs them, responds to them, entertains them, makes demands on them – and loves them unconditionally?

You can just as easily take the reasons not to have a pet and turn them into the very reasons your parents may want – and even need – to have one. Loneliness, isolation, inactivity, obesity, depression, grieving: Each in its own way can be partially, if not fully, alleviated by having a pet.

Kelly Connolly, Issues Specialist with the Humane Society of the United States (HSUS), made the case this way in the December 2005 issue of *Minnesota Monthly* magazine:

> *"Emotionally, pets can bring new meaning and purpose to the life of a senior who is living far away from friends or family. The love and commitment to their owners is almost like free therapy. They can act as friends, entertainers, and warm, fuzzy bundles of joy. Having a pet in an elderly person's life can offer them a sense of well-being, a sense of encouragement, and even a reason for living. Being responsible for another life often gives new meaning to the lives of those who are living alone or far from loved ones. Caring for and providing a loving home to a companion animal also helps elderly people to remain active and stay healthy."*

HSUS has a program to help bring animals together with seniors. Many local animal shelters also offer senior programs. Shelters have a number of advantages over pet stores. For starters, the shelter is more likely to have a staff that can advise and guide the potential new pet owner. Adopting from a shelter is also more cost-effective: Adoption fees are extremely low compared with the cost of purchasing an animal

Animal Therapy

Lois, a colleague I used to work with in senior housing, recently got a new dog. Baily is a funky Heinz 57 mix of Schnauzer with overly large ears. He's lucky enough to go to work with her – and the residents and staff at her community benefit greatly.

Lois had me close to tears when she told me about one of Baily's recent "patients." Alice, a resident at her center, usually doesn't speak much. She's blind and confined to a wheelchair. One day, her son brought her down to see Baily. Lois asked the son if she could put Baily in his mom's lap. The son asked mom and she said yes.

Now, Lois was a little worried because Baily had just been racing around, playing, and Lois wondered if this was a good idea after all. But as soon as she put her rambunctious dog onto Alice's lap, Baily melted. Alice wrapped her arms around him and began talking softly to the dog. And there they sat ... and sat ... until the son said he needed to go.

"No, the dog is comfortable here," his mother replied as she continued talking to and petting this now mellow dog. Five more minutes, 10, and the son said again, "Mom, I need to get going." Again, Alice replied, "No, the dog is comfortable here." Finally, Lois coaxed Baily off Alice's lap and welcomed her to come back anytime for a little Baily loving.

There was a connection there between that dog and that woman. A friend of mine thinks Baily knew he had a little therapy to do and accepted the task. Alice has since recounted her experience to many other residents and staff. For her, this simple encounter provided lasting joy.

from a pet store or breeder. Typically, they'll include vaccinations as well as spay or neuter procedures. And if mom and dad aren't really up for dealing with the training needs of a very young puppy or kitten, shelters have adult animals, many of them already house-broken and trained.

Part Of The Family

Of course, if your parents do have a pet, it needs to be included in any plans you're helping them make. If I ever became ill or unable to express my wishes, I would want professional staff and family alike to know that having Eli, our current dog, near me would be essential in my recovery. Do your parents feel this way about their pets? When they can no longer care for them, what do they want done? If you don't know, ask. Then write it down and put it in their "important documents" folder. Then make copies – for everybody.

Similarly, if they have to move from a home where they have a pet to one where they can't keep one, what are their wishes? Having to give up a pet at any age can be devastating. In your parents' later years, it can be especially tough.

Pets have an uncanny ability to radiate love. Not only did I bring along my dog, Paddy, to senior living communities in Denver, I often brought my bird, Spike, as well. He was always a hit. Some residents simply plunked themselves down next to the bird cage and had conversations with him most of the day.

Often, I'd "assign" them to look after Spike – making sure no one stuck fingers into his cage, and putting a blanket over the cage when it was time for Spike's nap. They took on such tasks whole-heartedly. Sometimes, these were the only activities that engaged them. They felt Spike needed them. I knew they needed Spike just as much.

Animals help us through physical and emotional illnesses. An effective tool in helping kids from abusive family situations is to put them together with animals. The kids learn unconditional love. They also learn that love doesn't have to hurt. Your parents can find similar benefits in having a pet in their lives. If they happen to live in a facility that forbids pet ownership, nothing says they can't volunteer at a local shelter or humane society.

If it's in walking distance, so much the better!

Parent-Directed Activities

For simplicity's sake, we've been talking about "parents" as though there are still two of them, and you're caregiving for both in approximately the same way. Chances are, this is not always or forever going to be the case. As they continue to age, their conditions may change and come to vary greatly, further complicating your role with the need to provide different forms and levels of care simultaneously.

In the best of circumstances, at least one parent will still be able to stay active and involved in a variety of activities without a great deal of oversight or assistance from you. In this section, we'll look at ways to focus that parent in particular on activities they can manage largely on their own.

First, I'll look at the important differences between staying busy for the sake of looking busy, and staying involved because of the important personal benefits that can be derived. I'll indulge a personal favorite, scrapbooking, for its potential to provide satisfying activity for your parents and important family insights for you, your siblings, and the generations that will follow. Finally, I'll outline an activity especially suited to just one parent's involvement: mentoring. It offers the greatest of rewards — their experience and values live on through another person — without requiring much involvement at all on your part.

CHAPTER 7

Staying Busy vs. Staying Involved: Self-Sustaining Activities

When I worked in senior-care communities, I remember many marketing folks asking me to have a big event going whenever they had a tour coming in. It was as if they felt they needed to distract families from the ordinary – that loud and colorful group activities outweighed smaller-scale interactions and private time for residents to pursue individual interests.

Family caregivers easily can fall into variations of a similar trap: Either thinking that the appearance of their parents being busy trumps the actuality of being involved in an activity that's engaging and meaningful to *them*, or thinking that – like some impromptu cruise directors on the Good Ship Getting Older – it's somehow now up to the *children* to constantly be planning activities for their moms and dads.

Don't get me wrong: There's plenty of value, mental and physical, in spending time with your parents to help them stay active and busy. But I believe it's the "slow times" and the hours when your folks are on their own, pursuing their own interests in their own ways, that provide the greatest payoffs for their emotional and bodily health.

The trick is to help them get into things they will find enjoyable over the longer term – including activities they might do solo, and under their own direction – because those are the ones they'll do regularly, and sustain by themselves.

Finding Fun

Whether they live independently in their own home, have an apartment or condo in a senior-living complex, or have moved to a form of assisted living, the more in control of their time and choices your parents feel, the better for their long-term physical and emotional health. That doesn't mean that activities planned and structured by others have no place in their lives. Rather, it says even greater benefits can accrue when your parents are active and take ownership of their own involvement in the various communities to which they belong.

In other words, when *they* decide they *want* to do something, it's fun. When *you* decide they *should* do something, it's maybe fun — but maybe also a source of friction between you.

Certainly, when their health and mobility place limits on them, they may need your help: setting up activities for them, getting them to and from those activities, and making sure the benefits they're receiving are worth the time and energy involved. But to the extent that you can point your parents toward forms of involvement that do not require your active participation or oversight, you're probably going to find that they have more interest in what they're doing ... and you have more time for other things.

The range of self-sustaining opportunities is virtually limitless. Here are a few broad categories:

Book clubs: Intellectually stimulating, but not physically taxing, these are organized groups that get together regularly to discuss a book the members have agreed to read. Beyond the chance to explore the book itself, they provide an opportunity for your parents to meet new people, who may or may not be their own age, and engage in active discussion (a great mental fitness workout). You can help your parents check out the various options offered by nearby libraries, colleges, community recreation departments, senior centers and private organizations to find one that feels right for their interests. For example, if they like a specific type of reading or literature, from history to cookbooks, encourage them to follow it. Eventually, perhaps with a discreet nudge, they may want to volunteer for a leadership role so the group continues to grow and evolve.

Story circles: Similar to book clubs, only the stories are told by members from their own experiences, typically all focusing on a predetermined topic, not read from someone else's book. According to Story Circles International (www.storycirclesinternational.com), telling and hearing personal stories is more than just fun and a relaxing good time. It engages the mind, validates participants as individuals, enhances self-esteem, and provides mental stimulation. When school children or family members are included, it also creates new forms of multi-generational interaction and mutual appreciation. The Story Circle Network (www.storycircle.org) is a clearinghouse designed specifically for women.

Food groups: For many of our parents, food is a wonderful connection point and can be a catalyst for a variety of activities, from volunteering to cook for community groups and events to participating in dine-out clubs that gather regularly to sample local cuisine. Food prompts group members to tell stories about their upbringing. It gives them a chance to share both conversation and concoctions with others. We preserve a lot of our cultural traditions through our favorite foods, from ethnic specialties to cherished family recipes. Worth noting: Encouraging your parents to get involved in food-oriented activities also is a discreet way to reinforce that they need to be eating regularly and well (a common worry for many adult children of aging parents).

Travel clubs: If they're going to sample foods of the world, why not go to the source? Travel is a common item on many seniors' wish lists – but too often it remains just a wish, in part because the idea of packing up and venturing off to places unknown all by themselves is a little daunting. The old bromide says there's safety in numbers, and it certainly applies in this instance. There's also fun to be had and new friendships to be made while participating in club-planned or group-sponsored tours, cruises and excursions that can range in duration from overnight to several weeks.

In Chapter 10, we'll explore travel in greater depth. For now, your parents may have their own ideas about where to go, but most likely will still value your help in choosing among options, obtaining passports and (if appropriate) international driving permits, figuring out currency and other "local" differences, and keeping an eye on things back home for them. If they've ever expressed a wish about going "back to the old country" or seeing something new, now's the time.

Exercise or walking clubs: As noted in Chapter 6, it doesn't take much time to achieve measurable health results from walking – just 30 minutes of physical activity several times a week. Involvement in a fitness group, and the peer pressure that often goes with it, can help your parents stick with an exercise program they otherwise might find too easy to let lapse. The trick is finding a group where they feel like they fit in. Once they make a friend or two (and discover they can keep up, and sometimes even set the pace), they'll have a new network of friends and a regular routine that doesn't require your presence.

In most areas, you won't lack for physical fitness alternatives: As our population progressively ages, community and private organizations of all types – park and rec departments, YMCAs, private health clubs, adult living communities – are targeting their activities to those at different ages and in different physical conditions. Programs for seniors are an important part of that mix.

Fun and games groups: Playing cards, playing golf, square dancing, gardening, crafting, quilting, painting, community theater – whatever they like to do, there's probably a group of people in the community who share the interest. On their own, you may find your parents seem strangely reluctant to do a lot of looking for such outlets. Suddenly, it's like they're back in junior high: self-conscious, awkward, not knowing who the cool kids (in this case, cool seniors?) are, and wondering whether they'll fit in. Have a little patience, but be willing to persist and support them. Provided you're helping them find forms of involvement that play to their interests, you can expect long-term benefits that will make your time searching well-spent.

A Sense Of Community

As Boomers, we're accustomed to playing active roles in our communities. Our parents may not be, or may be many years removed from the days when they felt comfortable with active outside involvement. In some cases, they may even feel the community doesn't want, or won't respect, their contributions. In this era of diminishing community resources and broadening community needs, that's a stereotype worth challenging.

What exactly is "community"? And where do your parents fit in?

🌀 Community is their neighbors, whether they live in a single-family home, an apartment or condo building, or an adult-living complex.

@ Community is the senior center, an independent- or assisted-living facility, or continual-care center.

@ Community is a church, synagogue, mosque or temple.

@ Community is a business, professional or philanthropic network.

@ Community also is family – from which too many seniors feel cut off because they can't match the busy go-go-go pace.

Some communities are formal, others casual. Some are easily seen (like the Red Hat Ladies), some all but invisible (like crisis counselors and shelter workers). Some are new and searching for recruits, others well-established but always looking for new members. Regardless, any and all can be vital connecting points that allow your parents to stay involved in a meaningful community, yet do so on a level that fits their needs and realities.

Looking for a place to start? In any city or town, good places include the local Senior Center, Council or Area Agency on Aging, Aging Services, and similar organizations.

For your parents – let's be honest, maybe for us, too – these are simple, but not easily established relationships. It's much easier to stay home, safely cocooned in our comfort zones. Don't. Challenge your parents. Challenge yourself. Find large and small ways to help them reach out, make contact, then get past the inevitable newbie stage until they feel part of what's going on around them.

If you're unsuccessful in helping your parents locate a group that fits their needs and interests, encourage them to start one. Odds are, there are others in the community who also are looking for opportunities to stay active and engaged. It only takes one or two recruits to provide the critical mass for a functioning activity group.

Making "The Move"

One of the underlying threads in this book is the unstated assumption that you'll do most of your caregiving in your parents' home (or your own). That won't always be the case – and it's not necessarily the dire prospect it may appear to be, especially in the context of our discussion of community. Keep an open mind.

Sometimes, institutional care is an improvement for both the care receiver and the caregiver. As long as your parents' needs are relatively minor and manageable, you can take them on with some degree of confidence. But advancing conditions – dementias, diseases in which physical and mental deterioration progress steadily, brittle bones, deep depressions – are typically going to be more than even the most dedicated and self-sacrificing adult children can handle effectively. That's where the professionals come in. And for some seniors, transitioning to a community where they're surrounded by their peers literally is a good move.

Re-Thinking The Unthinkable

I have always coached seniors to refrain from saying to their spouses or children, "Don't ever put me in a nursing home." It's a terrible burden to place on loved ones. Senior housing, assisted living, and ultimately nursing homes can allow spouses, children, extended family and friends to be with an aging adult without having to do the heavy caregiving. Meanwhile, that care can be provided by people who have chosen and trained to work in this vital but difficult field.

Despite what we hear in the media or over coffee with friends, these can be good places for your parents to live. There are bad ones, true. When you're taking a tour of a community, don't just talk with the marketing folks. Meet with the activity staff, aides and other residents. Watch and listen to how residents interact with the staff. Use your nose as well as your eyes and ears.

While you're doing that, note an often-unappreciated upside: The professionals who will be caring for your mom or dad in a care community don't have the emotional baggage you do. They don't have the buttons your parents may have become uncomfortably capable of pushing. Instead of constantly remembering your parents as they were in their younger years, they get to know them for who

I knew I couldn't move in with my Mom as her Huntington's advanced; she would only allow my Dad to help. He had accepted that role. At one point, when he was considering alternatives, he did visit a senior-care center. But, as is the case so often, when he actually confronted the changes such a move would bring to the basic circumstances of their lives, he ran away from it as fast as he could. For them, keeping Mom at home was the right choice.

On the other hand, after Eric's Dad had a stroke, followed by difficult surgery, a few years ago, his Mom chose to have him stay in a nursing home rather than attempt to bring him home. She knew her limits – both emotional and physical – and the level of his care had

they are today and care for them on that basis.

Just the same, always speak up when something is not right. Remember, aides get their orders from the charge nurse and usually have a multiple-patient load, so they may not be able to respond immediately to your requests. But they'll appreciate it when you give them first crack at solving a problem.

When you feel you need to take it to the next level, talk with the charge nurse or the social worker, or even the administrator. If you visit a care facility and the room smells, or your parents need to be cleaned up and changed, tell someone immediately. Tell several someones even – not to embarrass them or get them in trouble, but rather to get the care your loved ones deserve.

Sometimes, care communities can be that "home sweet home" both you and your parents desire. Most care workers have wonderful hearts. Like us, they aren't perfect in their caregiving. In the healthcare pecking order, aides are low-wage workers, yet they are routinely asked to provide a tremendous level of comfort as well as service. My advice: Compliment them. Talk with them. Bring pizza in for the night shift, or fruit for the day shift. Let them know you appreciate their work.

reached beyond *her* abilities. It was a difficult decision for her, the more so when an aide told her, "He doesn't need to be here. You should take him home." No one can judge our ability to provide care for a loved one – and no one should ever equate not providing care to not caring at all.

The toughest issue for Dick's dad to face when his wife's dementia became more than he could handle at home was accepting that her care truly was more than he could handle. His children were vocal – and unanimous – in supporting his decision, emphasizing that he would do neither himself nor her any good if he destroyed his own health trying to take care of their mom.

In some ways, Dick's mom has thrived in "memory care." She's eating better and more regularly. She's more active physically. She's more stimulated mentally. She's still in mid-stage dementia; that hasn't changed – and won't. But she's doing better overall than she was at home. And Dick's dad is healthier and less stressed, still living independently in his 90s.

It's difficult to place our loved ones in institutional care. The loss of place, the loss of privacy, the loss of individual control and some level of personal dignity and autonomy are so significant, many of us determine to do anything we can to put it off for as long as possible. Frequently, that's too long.

Combining your caring with the care that dedicated staffers take justifiable pride in providing can help your parents live their final years in as much physical and emotional comfort and security as possible.

And isn't that exactly what we want for them?

The Elderhostel Experience

I was asked to teach at my first Elderhostel in 1989. It was a Norwegian Language and Culture Week held at the Concordia Language Village site in Bemidji, Minnesota. I had just graduated from St. Olaf College and had no idea what an Elderhostel was, how I needed to prepare, or what the "students" would be like.

Because I didn't think old people could learn (an outrageous myth I've since spent a lot of my life trying to eradicate), I didn't prepare for my class in Norwegian. When I showed up, I had a roomful of eager students, waiting to learn verb conjugation and sentence structure so they could write to their relatives in Norway. These "hostelers," as they are sometimes called, were nothing short of amazing – full of life, a zest to learn, and enough energy to stay up talking and dancing into the wee hours. I left my first Elderhostel week so touched, I decided to do something with my life that included working with older adults. I have.

Elderhostel is America's first, and the world's largest, educational travel organization for adults 55 and over. Each year, nearly 175,000 adults sign up for some 8,000 programs offered in all 50 states and more than 90 countries. Most of this nonprofit organization's U.S. programs are either a week long or take place over a weekend. For those who want to travel abroad, there are multiple-week programs.

As the organization explains on its website (www.elderhostel.com):

> *"We believe learning is a lifelong pursuit that opens minds and enriches lives. We believe sharing new ideas, challenges, and experiences is rewarding in every season of life. Our participants come from every walk of life to learn together, to exchange ideas, and to explore the world. From Paris to New Orleans, Delhi to Council Bluffs, Elderhostel offers unique educational experiences infused with the spirit of camaraderie and adventure that enrich, and enhance, the lives of its participants. Our expert instructors share stimulating information through in-depth lectures, field trips, and cultural excursions. Lively discussions with faculty and fellow participants illuminate issues and broaden horizons."*

You bet I'm biased when I make a point of recommending this form of activity for your parents – and for you. Since 1990, I've been directing the Norwegian Language and Culture Elderhostel for Concordia Language Villages. Learning a language is a great way to work out the brain while getting to know another culture. If you become proficient as a result, so much the better. We definitely share new ideas, challenge old beliefs and learn from each other during these weeks. (And these days, I'm much better prepared!)

The camaraderie that builds is difficult to explain. Much of it has to do with the emotions older learners are so willing to express.

During lectures and discussions, it's not uncommon for participants to object, correct, interject their own life experiences, or clap with enthusiasm when they agree with points made. (How many educational experiences in your past involved spontaneous applause?)

It's a delight to see single men and women pair up, even if just for the week. Many widows have told me they feel safe and included when they travel on an Elderhostel. It's a true expression of people's lifelong experiences, combined with their love for learning and their sheer willingness to share of themselves.

Originally, most Elderhostel weeks were conducted on college or university campuses (typically when classes for traditional students were not in session). Today, many are held at hotels. Each setting has its advantages and disadvantages, but both emphasize hanging out after hours and informal interaction. It's also typical for Elderhostels to have a talent evening, which is often a rare treat … and a hoot!

Over the years, I have noticed one other interesting change: Participants attending my Elderhostel week have gotten both younger and older. When I started, most of my hostelers were in their 70s. Today, I have 50-year-olds trying to sneak in and 90-year-olds asking for unique accommodations. I love the different generations, though it does pose a challenge: Older attendees tend to be okay with (and some prefer) lecture-style presentations, while younger participants want active discussions.

It makes for a wonderful study of generational differences. And cultures. One of my favorite Elderhostel experiences involved a group that was celebrating Christmas during its week – and had two Jewish couples in the group. They were exploring, learning and extending their own comfort zones. Wonderful!

CHAPTER 8

Organizing The Past: Scrapbooking Combines Hobby And History

Some people look at a scrapbook and see simply a photo album: random pictures collected and stuck to a page, with no real thought or planning to it. Today, there's a whole lot more involved.

Actually, Mark Twain gets credit for first using the term "to scrapbook" as a verb (in an 1879 letter to his wife), and he even invented and patented a self-pasting scrapbook. The old guy would surely be amazed to see how the practice has grown. By some accounts, scrapbooking is the fastest growing hobby in the U.S. today.

These days, scrapbooks can entail journaling (telling the story behind the photos), memorabilia (tickets, letters, keepsakes, etc.), and highly focused forms of family genealogy. They can be interlaced with video and audio tapes to provide a form of family oral history. They can be developed around a theme, created to give each sibling a sense of his or her own personal story, or compiled as a lasting record of your parents' lives.

The process can be simple or complex. The "scrapper" chooses. In essence, each scrapbook is uniquely personal, a form of permanent record for the creator and a true gift to the person looking through it. If you're working with your parents, you'll find the time naturally evolves into reminiscing about people and places. If they're working on their own, they'll likely find scrapbooking can fill many a busy hour – and lead to many more when they page through their finished creations with you and other family members.

Both the activity and the memories can be very good for them. In addition to using fine motor skills and hand-eye coordination, building scrapbooks can give your parents a sense of accomplishment, help them chronicle their thoughts and feelings, and challenge their brains to put things together in both new and familiar ways.

Don't be surprised, however, if the process confounds some family mythology – yours as well as theirs. Hmm, looks like it was Uncle Everett who had that first-year Edsel, not Uncle Jake. And gee, according to this picture, there weren't any raspberry bushes behind

Going Negative

If your parents' photos are fading, or a significant number have gone missing over the years, don't overlook the negatives. In fact, a good way to preserve irreplaceable family photos is to have new negatives of them made and store those new negatives in a safe place. Or have the pictures digitally scanned.

Compared to pictures, negatives can be stored much more easily. Yet, even after years, they turn out new prints as crisp and bright as the originals. Although they're affected by fewer damaging agents, they're still vulnerable, however: to acids in an envelope, the gum adhesive on the flap, even chemical residue on pictures! The acid in a fingerprint also can potentially damage a negative, so always handle by the edges. Photo stores sell supplies that allow you to clean dirty negatives, and some have specialists who can repair or restore negatives that have been damaged over the years.

For best results, store negatives in PVC-free plastic sleeves that allow you to see what's on them without touching the image. Some sleeves are three-hole punched so they can be organized in a binder. If there's a place on the sleeve, make a note of the subject of the pictures and when they were taken. Someday, your kids may be trying to figure out what they're looking at.

Aunt Mart's garage; you must remember picking them at Cousin Mildred's across town!

In your parents' later years, scrapbooking can be a great way to connect your family across multiple generations, preserving memories in ways that resonate with you, your children, *their* children, and future folks yet to come.

Rescuing The Past

Start by recognizing that your parents' assortment of albums, framed photo collages, home movies, souvenirs, and shoeboxes full of photos and negatives, currently stuck away in odd corners, is anything but clutter. They're your family's history! Way too often, one generation's memorabilia is the next one's junk – tossed into storage or, worse, thoughtlessly consigned to the dumpster rather than recognized for the family heritage it represents. Now, perhaps left untended for decades, this irreplaceable resource could be decaying to the point where soon no one will be able to figure out what's left.

One of the more valuable, and enjoyable, activities you can engage in with your parents is helping them sort through and find ways to organize, preserve and expand all this stuff. It'll give you – and your children and their children – new insights into who you are, where you came from, and what your family has lived through and contributed to in decades past. And it will give your parents a focal point around which to organize and re-energize their memories.

First, assess the current state of what they have. In the past, many families commonly used "magnetic" albums or glue-faced pages that we've since learned can harm the pictures stuck to them so many years ago. Acid-carrying papers also destroy images. Those need to go. You may find images where the colors are fading or changing, the legacy of cheapo developing services. Do your parents still have the negatives? (See box, opposite.)

The good news is, times have changed. The papers and accessories available at scrapbooking and hobby shops, many department stores, and over the Web, offer all kinds of creative options for organizing family memories. Acid-free and lignin-free papers and adhesives can preserve photos safely for decades to come. Low-cost digital scanners allow old images to be copied to CDs and DVDs that are relatively impervious to fading and decay. Digital photo frames and albums are a fast-growing phenomenon. And "crops" – scrapbook events held everywhere from local retailers to multiple-day camps at fancy resorts – are attracting a growing number of folks, including Boomers and their parents.

I have always been a scrapbooker of sorts, but I was first introduced to the real difference when I was in Norway in 1985. Leafing through my Norwegian friends' photo albums, I was struck by the way they routinely cut, glued and embellished their pictures into scrapbooks instead of just sticking them in the plastic pockets of an album. If they went to the theater with friends, there was a photo of the group next to the theater, with glued ticket stubs, a program, and sometimes even a candy bar wrapper or other such memorabilia.

Because the cardstock backdrop was not covered in plastic, they also would write short stories or poems, or jot down their thoughts from the evening. Some scrapbooks didn't close perfectly because their creators had glued in dried flowers or a ribbon as decoration. I found them delightful.

I have a hosteler named Sandy who has been coming to my Elderhostels for 10 years. She is our resident photographer, and will often send me duplicates of the countless pictures she takes. She has been on two trips to Norway with me, and each time has created a marvelous retelling in pictures. More to the point, she's talented at putting her photos into albums that might better be called storybooks. What she'll give to her children and grandchildren is invaluable: her adventures, what she loved doing, the importance of her heritage, and a timeless sense of her adventurous spirit.

Not Junk – History!

Pictures aren't the be-all and end-all of scrapbooking. Almost anything can provide grist for a meaningful project. My Dad has a stack of playbooks and scripts from plays in which he acted many years ago in high school and the Red Wing (Minnesota) Summer Playhouse. He's got pictures, too – and, as a result, we've got family memories. I've told him I'd love it if he put together a scrapbook of the dreams of his youth and how they changed through the years. This would tell me how his priorities evolved and developed throughout his life.

When I created my wedding scrapbook, I glued in cards, music we sang, poems we had read, dried flowers from our bouquets, material from our dresses, etc. It's a very tactile, fun, lively reminder of my wedding day.

Dick once worked as a magazine editor. He recalls editing a story from a travel writer who made a point of bringing back menus from restaurants all over the world. They helped her call up very "flavorful" memories of her travels. Others who wander the world tie their memories to cups, spoons, bells, hat pins, postcards, even matchbooks.

Dick and his wife have their own very personal memory collection. They first met as pen pals, and they each saved the letters, cards and cassette tapes the other sent through more than two years of correspondence. Someday, their children will have that priceless form of family history to treasure, including their original letters, which hang in a sealed keepsake box on the wall of their bedroom. How surprised would you be to find your parents have something similar?

Learn The Craft

Basic scrapbooking materials include the album itself, plus background papers, photo corner mounts (as well as zots, sticky dots, acid-free glue sticks, etc.), scissors (which come in endless varieties), art pens, pigment-based inks (which are fade-resistant, colorfast and often waterproof), and mounting glues.

More elaborate designs call for more specialized tools, such as die-cut templates, rubber stamps, craft punches, stencils, inking tools, eyelet setters, embossing powders, heat embossing tools, and personal die-cut machines. (These last items, similar in size to a printer, can be connected to a home computer to cut any shape or font.)

Then there are the accessories used to decorate scrapbook pages, which scrappers call "embellishments." They include stickers, rub-ons, stamps, eyelets, brads, chipboard elements in various shapes, alphabet letters and ribbon.

The Scrapbook Process

As an enthusiastic scrapbooker, here are the steps I've learned to take.

1. Gather your materials. Look through all those shoeboxes or fancy photo storage containers, sort through the envelopes stuffed in various nooks and crannies, rummage through the boxes of memorabilia, or print things off your computer if you've taken to scanning fragile items to digital forms of storage. You may have to remove photos from albums, very carefully in some instances.

2. Sort, organize and label. Dating can be one of the most frustrating steps for a scrapbooker, but knowing the "when" adds definite value. I organize my photos in time periods or by subject matter – trips, college days, Elderhostels, etc. My Dad's second wife organizes linearly. Don't get hung up on the exact date – just an idea of the timeframe can be enough to put it in perspective. (And maybe someone looking at the scrapbook someday will help nail down fuzzy details more definitively.)

3. Choose a theme. Once you've taken stock of the photos, and other materials if they're to be included, you can help your parents plan the actual scrapbook project. Maybe it's a travel album of the family's vacations. Or an album of their grandchildren, assembled from grandma and grandpa's point of view. Or the wedding album they never had the time or inclination to do before now. Encourage them to think about what they want to pass on to the next generations through their scrapbooks, and – if they need the assistance – help them add those "words of wisdom" or lessons learned as part of the books.

4. Choose an album style. Scrapbooks come in all different shapes, sizes, weights, colors and styles. You can browse stores or take your parents online to gather ideas. An outing to a scrapbooking store can be a great way to focus your parents on the end result and show them just how many options are out there beyond the old black mounting corners and rubber cement. Even better, if they have the interest and you have the time, take a scrapbooking class together.

5. Create the album pages. There are as many layout possibilities to choose from as there are scrapbookers. You can find predesigned formats to follow, make up your own as you go, or invent some

Tips And Techniques

Words plus pictures: Second only to the photographs themselves, journaling is a vital part of scrapbooking. The style can vary, from short to long, objective to highly personal, but this is what separates a scrapbook from just another photo album. Here's a little bit of family immortality to work with: Long after their voices are gone, your parents can still speak to you through the pages of a scrapbook.

Extras: When you find several copies or several versions of a picture, don't immediately discard the ones you don't use. I make cards out of those "extra" photos and send them off for others to enjoy, sometimes adding stickers or stamps to create hilarious greetings for all occasions. People love them! Or you could put them in a grab box for siblings and others to pick through. Could be a brother or sister would like some for a collage, or a grandchild can use a few for a school project.

Black-and-whites: An unexpected way to preserve old black-and-white photos is to make color copies of them. It may seem strange, but you'll capture the shades and shadows more clearly.

Identifications: As you're going through pictures with your parents, make a point of having them identify everyone they can – including not just given names, but nicknames, special interests and even long-forgotten quirks that may provide context. Listen (or ask) for extra details, too: When the pictures were taken, where, what the occasion was, what was going on, what happened to the people or the places in later years.

Organize thyself: This is a good time to take pity on your children, who someday may be going through the same exercise with you. My Dad's second wife has taught me the importance of dating and labeling photos immediately. If you have a camera that puts a date stamp on the photo, so much the better. We think we'll remember, but chances are, we won't.

combination that works for you. If you (or they) are new to the craft, however, start simple. It's easy to be overwhelmed by the wealth of possibilities available.

6. Assemble and share. Make sure you include the backstory of the scrapbook: Who created it, when, perhaps even to whom your parents would like it given eventually.

Your Back Pages

Visuals, from pictures to other tactile pieces of our pasts, can evoke strong feelings. Through them, we bring back memories, experiences and lessons learned that helped shape our character, guided our actions and influenced our outlook on life in general.

Within my scrapbooks, I can choose not just the pictures that will memorialize an occasion, feeling or thought, but how those pictures will be cropped, captioned and displayed. (Yes, I said "cropped" – it's quite okay to physically cut things to different sizes and shapes if that helps them tell their story more effectively.)

I can decide on the mood and feeling of the page by varying the color, changing the design and adding words (a few or many, depending on the subject at hand). And each scrapbook I do is a brand new beginning, a new chance to create and chronicle in a different way.

There is no right or wrong way to do it, so any scrapbook will be a success. Plus, the results are just plain pretty!

CHAPTER 9

Active Aging One-On-One: Your Parents Are Never Too Old To Be Mentors

"Why did you do all this for me? I don't deserve it. I've never done anything for you."

That's Wilbur the pig questioning Charlotte the spider in the beloved children's book, *Charlotte's Web*, by E.B. White (1952, Harper & Row, by some calculations, the best-selling children's book of all time). In case you don't remember (or know) the story, Charlotte is the one who teaches Wilbur the ways of the barnyard and helps him become the prize pig at the fair, rather than an evening supper. Nothing in their individual natures provides a rationale for that role.

Charlotte's reply? "You have been a friend…. By helping you, perhaps I was trying to lift up my life a trifle. Heaven knows anyone's life can stand a little of that."

The role Charlotte plays for Wilbur is that of a mentor, a perennially trendy term in the business world and some imaginative civic communities as well. Despite such modifiers as age and physical condition, it can be an excellent way for your parents to stay active and connected, and feel rewarded for the experience and wisdom they've accumulated through their lifetimes – especially if one is able to be more active than the other, and needs some stimulating outlets.

If you're providing care to a parent who has lost their spouse, involvement as a mentor can be a way of getting them out of their shell – or keeping them from withdrawing into one in the first place. Even better, they may be amazed by how much their own spirits and health are lifted by playing an upbeat, positive role doing a little not-too-heavy lifting for others. Best of all, your involvement can be relatively low-key: encouraging them to get started and stay involved, perhaps providing some periodic transportation or other support, and reinforcing their commitment with regular positive feedback.

Defining The Role

Just as Charlotte does for Wilbur, the key to a positive mentoring relationship is for the mentor to assume responsibility for the development of something for the mentee, (sometimes referred to as the protégé). The mentee's responsibility is to listen to and trust the mentor. It's not a quick fix or a one-time thing: *Charlotte's Web* not only tells a touching story of a mentoring relationship, it beautifully illustrates how a mentorship takes time to build.

Yes, but what about the age factors involved if your parents get into mentoring relationships? What if someone … gasp … dies? One more reason *Charlotte's Web* is such a remarkable model: Charlotte eventually does die, but Wilbur, though saddened, is prepared for it and able to deal with it.

The fact is, mentoring relationships can work in virtually any age combination. Whether your parents are younger, older or of the same age compared to their mentee, it's the interaction around some form of personal development that provides the linkage.

Most often, we think of mentoring in the workforce, when a more seasoned employee gives advice and guidance to a younger colleague. But each life stage provides opportunities:

- Helping a child learn how to get along with friends, or deal with the loss of a parent, or master a skill or craft (including basics like reading and math).

- Giving an adolescent a supplementary source of advice and encouragement at a difficult stage of life.

- Offering support and guidance to an inexperienced or overwhelmed parent (there's a reason television's "nanny shows" struck such a responsive chord).

◉ Coaching a peer through family or health transitions, or helping them adjust to a major change in their living circumstances, or – perhaps from personal experience – working with them as they deal with the death of their life's companion.

While there's something of a one-way dimension in terms of what we might label power or authority or expertise, mentors receive definite benefits in return. As teachers know, there's a wonderful sense of pride and pleasure in seeing someone make use of newly imparted knowledge and skills – and feed back gratitude to the source. For mentors sharing their knowledge (of literature, of history, of how to run a business, of whatever), the mentee's interest and enthusiasm can, in turn, provide inspiration to be more adventuresome, or more self-assured, or more proud of their life's accomplishments.

Introducing The Idea

You'll want to give some thought to this before you bring it up with mom or dad. Simply blurting out, "Hey, ever thought of being a mentor?" isn't likely to prove very productive.

This definition from *The Elements of Mentoring*, by W. Brad Johnson and Charles R. Ridley (2004: Palgrave Macmillan), may be a good one to share as a starting point: "Mentoring relationships (mentorships) are dynamic, reciprocal, personal relationships in which a more experienced person (mentor) acts as a guide, role model, teacher, and sponsor of a less experienced person (mentee or protégé)."

Five Things Mentors Do

1. Point people in the right direction.
2. Provide information and supportive advice from their own experience.
3. Act as someone to talk to – someone who will understand things from "my (the mentee's) point of view."
4. Offer encouragement and a sense of progress.
5. Serve as a positive role model.

The more specific you can be in bringing the idea into play, the better. Look for ways to connect to interests or skills your parents enjoy and are proud of. Point out some of the benefits they've experienced when they were involved at work, or school, or church, or in community organizations in years past. Emphasize the degree of control they can have in setting limits: how many hours, devoted to what specific needs. Make sure there are no interruptions, so you can give time to their questions and doubts and objections.

If they're unfamiliar with the concept, or seem to struggle with relating the idea to their current circumstances, draw on their own experiences for examples. Who have been important influences or guides in their lives? Do they remember a special teacher who taught them a life lesson? A boss who was instrumental in their career success? What was the lesson – and how might their lives have been different if no one had been there to help them? Have them tell you about some of their role models and the characteristics that still make those individuals stand out in their memories (another way to get at life lessons learned from a mentor or guide).

Then ask them how, if there were no limits on them, and they could do whatever they wanted, they would want to draw on something that's important to them to add something to someone else's life? That's what can make them a good mentor.

Criteria For Success

It's natural to fear that taking on a role like mentoring could grow to consume more time and energy than they feel they have – or even blow up in their faces. Here are six criteria you can help them establish to assure that the experience is a good one for everyone involved.

1. Clearly defined goals. Mentoring should be *about* something. It's not an open-ended volunteer commitment, or a generalized friendship for that matter. If they're going to mentor someone toward becoming more physically active, for example, activity is the goal. They're not expected to give medical advice, or lead physical exercise or recreational activities, just listen to the fears and concerns of someone who is not as physically active as they want to be, and provide encouragement and tips toward that person's chosen goal.

2. Committed relationship. Knowing what mentors do and what their own personal strengths, skills and gifts are, they should choose someone to mentor who is both interested in, and a good fit for, the relationship. Do they share common traits? Do they see how they can teach and guide? Have they identified specific weaknesses to help strengthen, or skills to develop? Have they also agreed on how much time to commit? This last element will vary, but typically mentors meet at least once a month with their mentees, and both need to treat this commitment as a contract.

3. Productive mentoring skills. There is no great mystery to becoming a good mentor. Successful mentors usually have a genuine interest in helping others develop, plus the capacity to learn and adapt to changing situations. Useful traits and skills include:

- Relevant experience – Whether it's life experience, travel experience or work experience, mentors should be able to call upon knowledge gained from past situations.

- Good listener – Mentees often say that they just need someone to listen. If your parents have a tendency to lecture or preach, remind them of the importance of active listening skills: putting themselves "on a shelf," tuning into expression as well as words, listening with the eyes, showing positive body language (like leaning in and sitting in a relaxed position), paraphrasing thoughts and asking questions for clarification.

- Positive role model – It will help if a prospective mentee will not only look to your parent for advice and support, but look up to them as well.

- Supportive – Mentees will rely on their mentors to provide a supportive ear, coach them through the difficulties they may be experiencing, and find ways to spur them on when their motivation or confidence is at low ebb. If your parents are prone to judge quickly or criticize harshly, or lack basic patience and empathy, mentoring may not be a good choice. (But give them the benefit of the doubt: Who they were to you may not be who they will be to others.)

◑ Willing to learn – One of the worst things mentors can do is act as if they know everything. This is a common criticism of older adults especially. Good mentors know what they know, but also are willing to keep an open mind and learn something new.

4. Mutual benefits. Just as both the mentor and the mentee must be willing to listen and to talk – it can't be a one-way street, from either direction – both should benefit. Mentoring relationships should reward both participants with increased self-esteem, heightened vision, increased respect for diversity, and a new outlook on life events. If the relationship isn't working, it's best to end it rather than force it to continue, to the detriment of one or both of the participants. But, provided your parents have the temperament for it,

Centering On Seniors

When working with your parents to identify communities in which they can find meaningful involvement as mentors, don't overlook perhaps the most obvious one: assisting people their own age.

Many active seniors stay as far away from their area's nursing homes and assisted living communities as they can. It's too close to where they worry they could be someday. Yet nursing homes, in addition to being an often-neglected part of the larger community, are places chock full of people who share common memories and experiences with your parents.

Here's a chance to feel needed – and by people with whom it can be much easier to identify and relate. Sometimes, nursing-home residents just want someone to sit with them and listen to music or read. Other times, the friendship can be more active and structured, even therapeutic: from physical exercise to using Marge Engelman's Mental Fitness Cards.

I can tell you from experience how grateful the staff will be. There are never enough volunteers.

encourage them to try again. Sometimes, it's just not the right fit.

5. *Continuous evaluation.* Both parties should have goals, and both should be checking those goals regularly to gauge success. Oftentimes, I hear older adults say things like, "These young kids don't want to hear about my upbringing." To me, that's a sign that the relationship has gotten off-track: The mentor has become too wrapped up in storytelling to maintain focus on the mentee's needs, and the mentee doesn't have a good way to articulate why the stories aren't proving relevant. It might be time to revisit goals and either refocus on them, as originally intended, or revise them in light of changes since. It's also possible the mentorship itself has run its course. If the goals have been realized (or proven unreachable), it may be time to conclude the relationship.

6. *Consistent recognition.* Praise, praise, praise – relationships of all kinds thrive on positive feedback and reinforcement. Midway through *Charlotte's Web*, Charlotte and the other barnyard animals decide they need to tell the humans how wonderful Wilbur the pig is. They choose the word "terrific" and Charlotte begins to weave it into her web. "But I'm not terrific, Charlotte," Wilbur protests, "I'm just about average for a pig." Charlotte, deep into her mentoring role, replies, "You're terrific as far as I'm concerned and that's what counts."

We all need to be told we're terrific. Good mentors know that by giving praise, they're also lifting up their own lives. And no matter how much praise they're hearing from their mentee, they'll love hearing how much you respect them for what they're doing, too.

The investment is relatively low. The rewards can be very high – and long-lasting. If you're looking for a tactic that can help either or both of your parents continue to feel useful and valued, and without requiring a great deal of active involvement on your part, this is well worth considering.

Actually, re-reading *Charlotte's Web* might not be a bad way to pique mom or dad's interest in the idea of mentoring.

Finding Creative Outlets

It's one of the banes of retirement:

Compared to the work they've done all their lives, including raising a family, your parents may be feeling there's nothing stimulating to think about or do anymore. If they're adjusting to relying on you for care, that feeling may be magnified by a sense that they no longer can do things the way they used to, even if they still want to.

Wrong! Travel is one alternative that's readily available, and in ways that can be customized to physical conditions and personal needs. Hobbies are another. Then there's reading and the arts, from music to museums. Don't discount the value of lessons learned. Who knows? There could be a book in your parents – maybe more than one.

As you'll see in this section, there are a lot of things you can do within the context of caregiving to keep your parents from turning inwards on themselves. For starters, help them get out to travel the world, even if they have to do it vicariously. Turn to music for its ability to soothe and enliven. Inspire them to leave a highly personal legacy for your offspring – and generations yet to come – by capturing their basic principles and life lessons in the form of children's books.

They've spent a lifetime piling up experiences on the one hand, and things they wanted to do but couldn't on the other. Now's the time to tap one and indulge the other. Let me show you how.

CHAPTER 10

Reinflating The World:
There Are Plenty Of Ways
For Your Parents To Travel

Travel can be an uplifting source of excitement and adventure. Going to new places. Experimenting with new things. Trying new foods. Making new friends. Bringing home new memories. Or simply revisiting favorites from a lifetime of such experiences.

If you're actively into a caregiver role, odds are at least one of your parents is no longer physically able to travel – at least not the way they used to. But that doesn't mean their world has to close in to just the walls around them. Senior-oriented travel services are a growth enterprise worldwide. Various forms of media – books, brochures, videos, foreign films, especially the aptly named World Wide Web – can take them to faraway places. And by drawing on the personal insights of family, friends and total strangers the world over, even the most physically restricted can continue to experience the joys of travel in their later years.

In keeping with their age or physical condition, there are three basic ways for your parents to continue to travel. The obvious one is to get up and go. But sources both local and virtual can bring the travel experience to them. And they can travel vicariously through books, videos, television and even their own memories of trips past.

Get Out And Go

Going someplace feels like the ideal. For your parents, it can be a terrific use of time, and a terrific stimulant for their minds and their spirits. It could be the simple joy of revisiting a favorite place, whether that place is across the state or halfway around the globe. It could be the adventure of journeying to someplace new and different.

Whichever way their "traveling Jones" wants to take them (yep, Jonesers, we're talkin' about our half of the generation, courtesy of Lynyrd Skynyrd and "You Got That Right"), don't let your parents simply assume they've reached a point in their lives where getting away from home on their own is no longer an option. Maybe they got that right, of course. But if they've loved traveling in years past, it's worth helping them find out that they could very well be wrong.

Provided they have the interest, the mobility and the basic financial wherewithal, the odds of finding a way to get them where they want to go, and supporting them in however they need to be supported while they're there, probably are much better than they imagine. Travel and tourism represents almost $150 million an hour in economic activity in this country alone (more than a trillion dollars a year), and accounts for one out of every eight non-farm jobs in the U.S., according to the Travel Industry Association of America, so they're likely to find plenty of company.

And companies. The progressive aging of not just our country's population, but the world's, is giving birth to growing numbers of senior-oriented travel and tourism planners, even as it's changing the way buildings are constructed, streets and sidewalks are laid out, transportation is provided, and other services are delivered.

We've already discussed one option: Elderhostel. That's just for starters. When we typed "senior travel" into a search engine while preparing this book (November 2006), we generated more than 52 million returns! "Armchair travel" returned more than two million hits all by itself.

In a world that's changing so constantly, and so rapidly, it's beyond the scope of a book to list the most up-to-date travel resources. We've collected a few basic Internet addresses in the Resources Directory (see page 171), but check your local newspapers, senior centers, libraries, community and church groups, travel agencies, state travel and tourism departments, chambers of commerce, industry associations and, obviously, the Web for more. For international destinations, don't forget the embassies or local consulates of the countries your parents might want to visit.

Remember to look for "foreign" opportunities close to home. Most cities of any size, and lots of small towns, have a variety of heritage festivals and other celebrations throughout the year. They provide a chance to experience, or re-experience, the foods, the dress, the crafts, the history, the language of a new or favorite place – and without crossing a time zone line or lining up for a Customs check. These days, for example, I do a lot of my own foreign travel without ever leaving my home state of Minnesota via Concordia Language Villages' Elderhostels and other adult weeks and weekends with language and culture themes (www.concordialanguagevillages.org).

If you're helping set up trips or outings for your parents, be specific about particular conditions that need to be taken into account so they can travel safely and successfully: wheelchair access, special diets or accommodations, the ability to bring along an attendant. Many places will seat people with limited mobility or other physical handicaps first, or find ways to relieve them from the draining ordeal of standing in lines.

Airlines have wheeled chairs sized to fit down the narrow aisles of an airplane, and (since it smoothes the boarding process for everyone else) will be more than happy to help your parents get aboard and seated early. If one or both are on oxygen 24/7, most airlines – given sufficient notice – will configure a seat or two to provide access to the plane's oxygen system. (What did you think all those little drop-down masks you've ignored during preflight safety orientations by flight attendants through the years are connected to?)

Dick's late father-in-law spent the last 30 years of his life in a wheelchair with MS. He also traveled from his Iowa home to take in sights as diverse as Disneyland in Anaheim and a roller derby in San Francisco. Those travels, in turn, helped him stay upbeat and positive, even as the disease progressed.

Home, But Not Grounded

Armchair travel involves a lot more than just sticking in a video or DVD, or tuning in to a travel channel, though those can be pieces of the overall experience. Even better, it need not be a solo pursuit.

If your parents have friends with similar interests, suggest they set up their own little armchair travel group and meet periodically to

Traveling Healthy – And Smart

Before your parents hit the road, double check to make sure they're traveling smart – and that you're prepared to help them if they need you to.

Passports: By 2008, expect that (as with the rest of the world) a passport will be needed for even routine travel between the U.S. and Canada, Mexico, Central and South America, the Caribbean, and Bermuda. You should have your parents' passport numbers or a photocopy of their passports. You may also want to have duplicate copies of their birth certificates.

Health records: Anyone traveling should carry with them a list of their medicines (including dosages) and prescriptions (including eyeglasses and contacts), plus immunizations, known allergies, other physical conditions, and the phone numbers of doctors and clinics where they're currently being treated. You should have copies of that list. They may also want to take along a modest emergency kit: a small supply of over-the-counter medicines, including whatever they take for colds or allergies, Band-Aids and moleskin (the latter for blisters), extra batteries for hearing aids, etc.

Insurance: Make sure you have copies of their Medicare, Medicaid and private insurance cards, front and back, in case they lose their wallets or purses. If they purchase other kinds of coverage, such as trip-cancellation, or one-time riders for possessions, you should also have copies and notification numbers.

Credit cards: Similarly, make copies of both the fronts and backs of all the "plastic" your parents may be carrying, especially the theft and fraud notification numbers if something goes missing.

Emergency numbers: They should have several options with them, should something happen on the road – in particular, phone numbers that are likely to be answered by *real people* instead of infrequently checked voicemail. If they're carrying a cell phone, double check that the numbers programmed into the phone's memory are the most current ones.

compare their memories of places they've been, or explore places they'd still like to go. Here's a chance for them to share their pictures, slides, home movies, and souvenirs – stuff you've perhaps seen more times than you'd like to remember, but that they still get enthusiastic about.

Don't stop there. Armchair travelers can see and do plenty without taxing either their mobility or their finances. They can pop in a movie from or about the region or country to create a mood. They can add flavor by preparing a meal based on the cuisine of the place they're "visiting" (most bookstores have an aisle full of cookbooks, many of them focusing on ethnic foods). They can head out to a local restaurant that specializes in the foods of their chosen locale – or perhaps have food from that restaurant delivered.

While the catalog of great travel videos on the market continues to grow, I consider them starting points or icing on the cake, not focal points in and of themselves. Use the media components to set the stage before a visit, or a meeting, or an online excursion. But help your parents find ways to connect and interact with others. There's no replacement for mixing and mingling, however virtually or vicariously.

Example: For a "shared" travel experience, however offbeat, your parents and their armchair travel companions might decide to watch the same programming at about the same time. Then they can "meet" – face-to-face, by phone, or by Internet chat – to discuss what they've seen and how it compares to what they've previously experienced (or imagined).

To supplement videos and travel programs on cable, help your parents find people who have spent time there (wherever the chosen "there" is). In our increasingly multicultural world, odds are someone you know has roots in another region of the country or world. In fact, discovering people's roots could make for an interesting form of scavenger hunt. It's not like you're going to put someone on the spot by expecting a polished presentation. But you could certainly ask them to be on hand to answer questions or add personal stories to a video or other travel-oriented experience.

Traveling through books is another way to tap into the sense of adventure and discovery. A travel-oriented book club can be a venue through which your parents both add to their travel experiences and interact with others who have similar interests.

Perhaps your parents can still serve as travel resources for others in the community? Look for ways to match up their experiences, ethnic roots, language skills or other multicultural expertise with local groups that can benefit, from schools and churches to businesses and civic organizations.

Don't overlook the reverse option: having the travel (or more specifically, the traveler) come to your parents. When my uncle visited us from Kodiak, Alaska, a few years ago, he gave our family a rare glimpse not only of his home, but of his way of life. He's a commercial fisherman, has been for many years. But I'd never seen pictures nor understood much about the process until he came through Minnesota.

Happily for us, he brought along a picture CD and gave us a slide show on our laptop. We were able to see his processor boat and ask him countless questions. Ever since, my view of Alaska and the northern reaches of the Pacific has been vividly real. I understand why Alaskan cruises are so popular. From active volcanoes to huge eagles feeding on fish heads, I've seen my uncle's part of the world through his eyes, heard about it in his voice. We feel like we've been on his boat … even though we haven't – yet.

Traveling The Web

Maybe your parents can no longer leave home physically. That doesn't mean they can't "leave" in other ways. In today's wired world, they can still see exotic places, journey back to ancestral lands, meet new people, reconnect with old friends, and generally experience most of the sights and sounds (if not the smells) of travel – and all from the comfort of home.

One of the most important reasons for helping your parents achieve even a modest level of computer literacy is to give them access to the World Wide Web. Traveling virtually can help them stretch, learn and reach out in new ways, regardless of age or physical condition.

For non-computer-literate seniors, the Web can seem very intimidating at first click. Trust your parents to have heard, and believed, every scary story about Internet predators the evening news has breathlessly promoted. You can help them understand that, while there are some dangers, the Web really is no different than any other strange new place they might visit. You can get mugged in Rome, scammed in Cairo, lost in Tokyo, or taken for a ride in Rio de Janeiro. Provided you learn the lay of the land and take the most basic of precautions, you also can have a wonderful time there.

The same holds true for the Web. Through webcams, they can see and interact. Through a keyboard, which is much friendlier to arthrit-

Book It

The Travel Book: A Journey Through Every Country in the World (2005: Lonely Planet) is a wonderful resource for travelers, no matter how they want to see the world. So, too, is the organization's website, www.lonelyplanet.com, which offers travel resources and ideas, and serves as a virtual meeting place for travel enthusiasts worldwide (including a lively "Armchair Travel" section).

There's a clear philosophy at work:

> *"Lonely Planet is passionate about bringing people together, about understanding our world, and about people sharing experiences that enrich everyone's lives. We aim to inspire people to explore, have fun, and travel often. And we strive to provide travellers everywhere with reliable, comprehensive and independent travel information."*

Each of the United Nation's 192 defined countries is presented in words and pictures – not just statistics, but "Essential Experiences" (things to take in while visiting the country), "Getting Under the Skin" (what to read, listen to, watch, eat and drink), "In A Word" (a phrase from the country that may be heard often, or that encapsulates an essence of the country's spirit), "Trademarks" (typical things visitors will see or notice), and "Surprises" (preconceived ideas that may not be true).

ic hands than pens and pencils, they can correspond, journal and keep up with friends and family – especially computer-savvy grand-kids and great-grandkids. Because the computer "remembers," they can create a new record of their travels that they can leave to the family.

Present it properly and offer a little support (like helping them set up a high-speed connection, installing anti-virus software that updates itself, configuring their web browser, organizing bookmarks, and setting screen resolution and defaults in keeping with their vision), and the Internet can give your parents a brand new window on the world.

(If your parents reside in senior housing, be aware that there are professional companies that will help set up adaptive computer systems for them. Check out It's Never 2 Late (www.IN2L.com), which does wonders bringing seniors out of their cocoons and connecting older adults with grandchildren around the globe.)

To get his Mom, LoAnn, from an old dial-up configuration to broadband, Eric combined her budget with what she told him about how and where she intended to use an upgraded computer, printer and scanner. He also assessed her level of proficiency and willingness to learn new things, which told him he would have to take the initiative to get everything set up and configured.

He found products that matched her needs, then ordered the hardware and software, and contacted her cable provider to set in motion the service upgrade for high-speed Internet access (depending on the vendor involved, this can take several weeks and often requires installing additional gear). With the new components in hand and the connection ready, he took over her office space one afternoon to transfer her personal files and settings from a trusty but aging little Mac – unlike people and good wine, he likes to point out, computers don't age well – to a more elegant and powerful iMac.

After setting up and thoroughly testing everything, Eric had the pleasure of introducing LoAnn to her bright new window on the world. She had left the deliberative path of dial-up and zipped into the carefree lane of high-speed access. No longer would she be doing the dishes, laundry and other daily tasks while waiting for a website to load.

Plus, now her phone rings, even when she's online.

CHAPTER 11

Noteworthy Notes:
Music Always Speaks To Us

Music is a universal language. It can help us remember. It can make it easier to forget. It can take us to a relaxing space, lift our mood, get us dancing, soothe us to sleep.

For a caregiver, music can be an important ally as we try to support our parents emotionally. Through music, we can acknowledge that it's okay for them to feel sad, recognize why they're feeling sad, and then help them move through the sadness. We can remember the past, then refocus on the present. Through danceable music that's as wild or subdued as the situation calls for, we can defuse anger and channel energy. And we can make – or listen to and enjoy – the joyful noise that gives melody to happy times.

Even those who don't have a musical background benefit from hearing, playing and participating in music programs. The American Music Therapy Association (AMTA – www.musictherapy.org) promotes music's positive effects including: better memory recall, which contributes to reminiscence and satisfaction with life; upbeat changes in moods and emotional states; an enhanced sense of control over life; greater awareness of self and environment; management of pain and discomfort without (or with fewer) medications; opportunities to interact socially with others; and reduction of anxiety and stress for both older adults and their caregivers.

Caregivers also receive a variety of benefits: a forum in which to share common experiences and enjoyment; meaningful time spent together in a positive, creative way; intimacy through nonverbal interaction; respite and relaxation; and stimulation for family reminiscence.

Musical Mysteries

Music is huge for me, always has been. When I sang with the St. Olaf Choir, I got such a high during the concerts. I know I'm far from alone: Boomers may be the most diverse musical generation ever. We instinctively know that music can excite us or calm us, take us back or pull us forward.

How much more can this be the case for your parents? Many of them grew up in the era of radio, a primarily musical medium, not TV. They went to schools where music wasn't an add-on program – it was part of the everyday curriculum. Their musical education ranged over the classics of centuries – not just classic rock from the '60s and '70s and '80s.

How much do you really know about your parents' musical tastes, let alone their history? Try asking them sometime. For starters:

🌀 What role has music played in your life?

🌀 How does music affect you today?

🌀 What is your favorite type of music?

🌀 What's the most memorable concert or music event you remember – from your childhood, from when you were dating, from the war years, from when we kids were young?

🌀 Have you ever wanted to explore different genres of music?

🌀 Have you ever played a musical instrument? Or wanted to learn one?

Then listen and – even if you don't share it – respect their musical background and tastes. Use it as leverage in drawing them out on other, more difficult, subjects. Does it seem like they're always playing "the same stuff"? So what? There's comfort in familiar sights and sounds. Unless they're listening to the one and only CD or album in the house, it's probably okay.

While programming the monthly birthday party at an assisted

living community some years ago, I remember how the residents would continually ask for the same violinist to provide entertainment. The staff was tired of her, and even some family members complained about the lack of variety. But the residents loved hearing her, and requested her again and again. Rather than disenfranchise them, we made violin music a regular feature for birthday parties and found ways to mix in more variety elsewhere.

Powerful Forces

Even those who understand how powerful music is may not be trained to work with the emotions that emerge. I'm not a music therapist. I am, however, a trained musician who understands that there's a very valuable therapeutic side to music. According to AMTA, "Music therapy is an allied health service similar to occupational and physical therapies. It consists of using music therapeutically to address physical, psychological, cognitive and/or social functioning."

In *The Secret Power of Music* (1984: Destiny Books), David Tame explores music in four different contexts, each of which relates to health as well as harmony.

1. Music and the body. Have you ever wondered why restaurants play music? They understand it not only helps create a mood, but enhances digestion, stimulating the digestive system and helping the body assimilate nutrients. Research also suggests that the type of music can increase or decrease muscular activity, and make the listener's breathing either stronger or weaker, depending on how they react to what's playing.

Skin temperature is another bodily attribute that can change with exposure to music. In one classic study, 100 psychology students listened to music while their skin temperature was measured. Calming music increased skin temperature, music that aroused negative emotions decreased it.

2. Music and pain. Many studies have shown that music can be an effective treatment for pain. I remember when I'd visit my Grandma Gladys. Most of our visits would start off with going over her ailments – she suffered from frequent migraines as well as other aches and pains. But when I would play Benny Goodman albums on the Hi-Fi, we'd soon be re-visiting trips she and her husband had made to

Chicago to dance, or even dancing ourselves.

Music increasingly is being used in hospice care to reduce post-operative pain and control pain in general. The hospice team that cared for my Grandpa Gus in the later stages of his battle with bone and lung cancer included a music therapist to help soothe him, and we learned a lot about how music can change moods, even under the most difficult of conditions. When he was restless at night, for example, we knew to put on classical music to help him relax. It did.

3. Music and the brain. Music, especially playing or performing music, "wakes up" the brain. Specifically, it has an effect on brain-waves, the "rhythm" of our brains. Just as the heart and lungs have their own rhythms, so too does the brain. A rhythm means a wave: The more rhythm or brainwaves you produce, the more brainpower you create!

Several articles report that musicians produce significantly more alpha brainwaves than non-musicians. Alpha brainwaves (one of the basic four – delta, theta and beta being the others) are usually considered to reflect an "ideal learning state." When alpha brainwaves are active, we are said to be in charge, in a relaxed and effortless manner.

Here's where the language metaphor is especially apt: Learning to play a keyboard or another musical instrument has benefits for the brain similar to learning a new language. Joining a choral group, however informal, might offer another brain-boosting musical outlet.

Get Out Where The Music's Playing

Music can provide things to do with your parents – or things for them to do without you. Concerts are the obvious frontrunner, though pricing and transportation might be issues for some. But don't stop there. Find ways for your parents to get out to community band concerts and "music in the park" programs, musicals staged by local high schools and community theater groups, school and church programs (especially around holidays), even sing-alongs.

Because music engages different parts of the brain, energizing alpha brainwaves, your parents may very well notice that they are thinking and remembering things better. Plus, the experience is fun.

4. Music in daily life. Don't let your parents live trapped in silence. Too many times, I've been struck by the terrible quiet in the homes of seniors. From radio stations and satellite radio to CDs and special channels (helpfully segmented by type) provided by many broadband services, music is readily available, and at virtually no cost. Urge your parents to keep it turned on. It fills up the empty space, stimulates the brain, and can call up many warm and pleasant memories and emotions.

More specifically, the right music at the right time can pay big dividends. The list on the next page outlines 16 situations in which different kinds of music can play a helpful, healthful role.

Listen To Their Music

Ancient Chinese emperors believed that music provided a scientific method to take the pulse of the nation. Rather than looking at the efficiency of government, or getting expert advice on policy making, Emperor Shun would check the five notes of the ancient Chinese scale. Then he would listen to instruments and songs of the local regions, checking to see that they were all in tune with this basic five-note scale. When the Emperor traveled the kingdom, he would listen to the songs of the people. If the different villages were introducing "different" music, he took it as a sign that the unity of the kingdom was under threat.

Think about that in our culture today. Each generation seems to delight in complaining about the music of others. Too loud. Too slow. Too sweet. Too angry. Too boring. Too undisciplined. There may well be some truth to the generalizations. But there also may be some common ground that has gone unnoticed over the years – ground that now gives you a place to build a new foundation.

Here's a way to "get in tune" with your parents across the generational gaps. You can do this one-on-one, or two-on-two, or enlisting the grandchildren – any way is the right way. Your assignment: Each of you, independently, agrees to pick four different songs that fit into each of the following moods. The object is not to agree on four among you, but to compare each other's foursomes and find out more about each other in the process. The moods:

Slow, quiet and maybe a little melancholy: This is where we honor and come to terms with sad feelings. If you want something to play in the background, try Aaron Copeland's "Our Town," or "Nimrod" from Sir Edward Elgar's "Enigma" Variations, Op. 36.

A bit peppier, but still tranquil and mellow: These are songs that lift your mood and get your spirits soaring. One of my favorites is Dusty Springfield's version of "The Windmills Of Your Mind," in

Programming A Personal Playlist

 Here are 16 specific times and places where the music that's playing can change the tenor of what's happening.

Dealing With Emotions

Anger: Strong music releases anger, quiet music calms it.

Depression and fear: Music that will induce sleep for dejection and negative feelings; music from your faith, such as hymns, to provide reassurance.

Boredom: Big band or jazz can arouse new enthusiasm.

Strength and courage: Powerful music increases blood flow, speed of circulation, muscular energy and metabolism.

Special Times

Waking up: Beautiful, quiet pieces, perhaps music for strings or flute, to bring you back from sleep slowly. If you are prone to going back to sleep, choose peppier, brighter, airier styles.

Meals: Happy music, light and airy; avoid heavy, loud music and large contrasts. (Music that is pleasing to the ear heightens the taste buds, and sound, like flavor, helps to promote good digestion.)

Love and devotion: Music that can arouse understanding and fill relationships with joy.

which she starts off quietly intense, then kicks it up a notch.

Faster tempo and more upbeat mood – a toe-tapper: I enjoy the song "You'd Be So Nice to Come Home to," especially the version on the album Art Pepper Meets The Rhythm Section. Another great song is "When I Grow Too Old to Dream." I'm particularly fond of the version sung by Nat "King" Cole and His Trio.

Fast, lively and happy – makes you want to dance: One song that always does that for me is Tina Turner's "The Best." To hear over and over, "You're simply the best, better than all the rest" is also a

Insomnia: Quiet music for flutes, harps or strings makes a great substitute for chemical sleeping aids.

Accompanying Activities

Planning your day: Background music that is joyous, transparent and clear, not heavily orchestrated or dissonant.

Physical workouts: Peppy tunes, and music with stronger rhythms and powerful contrasts.

Hyperactivity: Quiet music, melodically pleasing, and slower in rhythm and pacing.

Children: Lullabies at bedtime are very soothing; in general, singing to children has a calming influence.

Setting A Mood

Home: Quiet music will treat stress, worry and high-strung states.

Relaxation and reverie: Quiet, perhaps nostalgic, music.

Clear thinking and mental power: Clear melodically and rhythmically; among classical selections, much of the music of the baroque period is ordered and melodic, with few surprises.

Humor: Fun pieces that help you unwind with a chuckle (think Dr. Demento – for your parents, Spike Jones).

wonderful self-esteem builder. (And you can dance to it.)

At this point you will probably have between 20 and 50 songs, maybe more than 100, depending on how many of you are doing this, how much or how little your tastes overlap, and how many "I really like this one but there wasn't room on my list for it" extras you've accumulated.

Don't file away the lists: Play them. Talk about them. Use them as a catalyst for other conversations. If there are particular pieces that your parents (or you) would like to have playing in the background in a hospital or hospice setting, make note of them now.

In addition, if someone (check the grandkids) has the interest and the computer skills, consider downloading the songs – fully respecting copyrights, of course – and creating a collection of family CDs for different moods that will be all the more meaningful because they contain *your family's* favorites.

The Key Of Life

Music can provide mental stimulation, spice up physical exercise, fill in the cold silences with warmth, and much, much more. It's a way to introduce your parents to new ideas and help them better understand the "younger generations." It's a way to share beauty and joy. It's a soundtrack for their memories – one that will endure as part of their legacy to you.

For your parents, and for yourself, when you want to support the emotions, recognize often-unvoiced needs and help them move through each day in an upbeat way, listen for the music.

CHAPTER 12

Leaving A Legacy: Writing A Children's Book

Okay, here's where we push the envelope a tad. Have your parents ever thought about writing a book? Well, why not? It doesn't need to be a major potboiler, like a John Grisham lawyer drama or a LaVyrle Spencer romance. How about something smaller in scale, a little more modest in style – but potentially very ambitious in scope? In short, a children's book.

So many times, we know our parents have things to say, but don't know how to say them – especially in a way that will reach future generations in their own words. When they feel a need to share their thoughts, their passions and their creativity with us, doing so through children's books is a fun, great way. Whether they want to take their story through to conventional publishing, or are content to turn to the growing number of print shops and copy centers that can self-publish a limited number for the family, it is the *activity* of writing that's important.

What's more, as we discussed in Chapter 3 in looking at how children's books can provide an access point for talking about touchy subjects, this is a great way for your parents to express how they feel about things – including the toughest and most emotion-laden issues.

Enticing The Muse

Your parents may find this idea outrageous on its face, or secretly intriguing. They may recoil at the thought or jump at it. The key is to limit your involvement to what they need to get going and stick with the project, then get out of the way and let them run with it.

It may be a matter of transcribing their handwritten material into a computer for reproduction. They may need help in determining how to lay out pages, or finding a printer that can handle a small-scale project. Sometimes, the most important role you can play will be as cheerleader – because even beguilingly short writing projects require a level of emotional commitment and self-confidence that inexperienced writers especially may be afraid to attempt.

One way to help them in the idea stage is brainstorming things to write about. Remember "the rules" of productive brainstorming:

🌀 The goal is quantity, not necessarily quality.

🌀 There are no bad ideas – all ideas are potentially good ones.

🌀 Ideas beget ideas – you never know what can percolate out of the most ordinary (or bizarre) suggestion.

🌀 No judging of suggestions at this point (that comes later).

For inspiration, ask your parents about their favorite stories – not books, necessarily, just stories. What stories did their parents (or grandparents) tell them in their own childhood to teach a lesson or illustrate a point? What idle daydreams have given them diversion or satisfaction over the years? What *bad* stories have they seen or heard – and thought, "I could do that way better?" Or think back to your own childhood: What stories do you remember them telling?

Once you have some "whats," probe for "whys": Why, after so many years, do these stories still call to them, or impress them, or even irritate them? Why do they feel strongly about some things – and what stories might they craft to pass on those principles and opinions to their grandchildren and beyond?

The Writing Process

Although experience and training help, the best way to write is to just write. Here are six basic elements that editors, reviewers and readers tend to look for in a story. They're suggestions and guidelines, not hard-and-fast rules. I know many writers who break them at will, though often they are very aware of why they're doing it.

1. Theme

A story's theme is an insight or viewpoint or concept that it's written to convey. To crystallize it, have them complete this sentence in 25 words or less: "The point of my story is _____."

Three tips for communicating a theme effectively:

Don't blurt it out. Let the theme emerge from the story. If they want to come right out and state it, do it in dialog, not in narration.

Avoid preaching. Children's stories should be explorations of life, not Sunday school lessons or "when I was your age" rants.

Keep it positive. If they're writing about a social problem – prejudice they've experienced or witnessed, say – the story should offer constructive ways for someone to deal with it, not a diatribe on why it's a problem.

2. Plot

Normally, a story is built around a conflict involving the main character: with another character, with circumstances, within himself or herself. A children's story doesn't necessarily need a traditional conflict, but it will need something else, another "plot device" that's designed to hold a child's attention.

Conflict often takes the form of a problem the main character must resolve. The character should succeed or fail at least in part through his or her own efforts. In realistic fiction, the character typically learns or grows in the process. The lesson or growth, in turn, conveys the theme.

In fairy tales, a staple in children's literature, there's no shortage of conflict, but things don't always have to conform to reality. If they look at a story such as *Cinderella*, your parents will find a familiar formula:

- Initial harmony – everything is hunky-dory. The main character lives well.

- Lack discovered – the main character notices something is missing in his or her life, which leads to …

- The quest – the main character takes off in search of what's missing, whether it be a tangible item or an emotional state.

◉ Magic enters – somewhere along the line, typically in the quest, a magical being steps in to help or confuse the main character.

◉ Conflict resolved – the magical element may help with the conflict or be the cause of it, but resolving the conflict concludes the quest.

◉ Moral or lesson learned – the key to a magic tale, and the thing your parents may hope to teach, or honor, or leave with generations behind them through their story.

What I've described above is called the Magic Tale Narrative Model. I learned it while studying for my master's at the University of Wisconsin, Madison. True magic tales are oral formulas, and usually

Four More Good Examples

 Countless children's books do a terrific job of combining style and substance. Four of my favorites:

Wilfrid Gordon McDonald Partridge by Mem Fox; illustrated by Julie Vivas (1989: Kane/Miller Book Publishers) – addresses the issue of Alzheimer's disease; beautifully written and easily understood.

The Lorax by Dr. Suess (1971: Random House) – an example of exposing an "issue" (in this case, pollution) in an approachable way.

Sofia and the Heartmender by Marie Olofsdotter (1993: Free Spirit Publishing; being republished by Holy Cow! in mid-2007) – a touching way to deal with parenting issues, mentoring, and how children learn to trust themselves.

The Keeping Quilt by Patricia Polacco (1998: Simon & Schuster) – describes the importance of family ties and how they are passed down to the next generation.

aren't intended to be written, but I think this model is a great system for your parents to use in writing a children's book.

I once taught it to a Brown Bag Lunch Bunch, a group of women, all of them over the age of 70. They used it to create a magic tale as a group, which they put on a cassette tape and sent to me. They were laughing and giggling throughout, so much so that they periodically had to turn the tape off. It's still a hoot to listen to.

A quick note about length: There often are several stages within the quest – arrival of conflict, initial success of the main character, reversals, final victory, and outcome. In a longer story, the success-reversal sequence may repeat. Children's books are designed for quick reads and short attention spans, so stick to the essentials. Also, a novel may have several distinct conflicts. A children's book, like a short story, should have only one.

3. Story Structure

At the beginning, jump right into the action. At the end, bring the story to a quick, clear close. In between, enhance reader interest by moving the plot forward with events and action, rather than with internal musings or talky conversational passages. Show the reader: Draw a picture in words instead of telling in tedious detail. Or illustrate the book with drawings, family photos and other images.

Keep the structure as simple as possible. In a children's book, action typically occurs in chronological order, without "flashbacks" that can confuse or distract younger readers. For a picture book story, it's important to include a number of locations ("scenes") to provide variety in the illustrations.

Children's books typically use either "first person" or "third person" voice for narration. In first person, the story is told by one of its main characters: "I did this." In third person, it's told as if by an outside observer: "They did that."

According to Aaron Shepard, a writer of children's books, "First person is popular with middle-grade and young-adult readers as it creates instant intimacy and can convey lively wit and emotion. But it can confuse younger listeners, so it should seldom be used in early picture books. Third person is fine for any age, and permits the writer more sophisticated language and observations."

Three Things Good Writers Know

Your parents may not have much experience as writers.

If their goal is to win a Newbery Medal (awarded annually by the American Library Association for the best children's books) or a Caldecott Medal (given each year to the artist of the most distinguished children's picture book), this might be an issue. If all they're looking to do is create a memorable keepsake for the family, on the other hand, it needn't be. Here are three things good writers know.

1. Just write. Don't worry about structure in the beginning. They can revise and polish a first draft, but they can't do a thing with an idea when it's still lodged squarely between their ears. There'll be time later on to correct the spelling, smooth out the phrasing, rearrange elements and paper over gaps in the story. For starters, the key is to get the essentials down on paper (or into a computer).

2. Start fresh. Writing new material right away rather than starting a session by first revising the last pieces they were working on will be more productive in the long run. Rationale: Using up scarce creative energy polishing something that's already written works against producing more material. The existing part gets better, but the manuscript somehow never seems to get any longer. Or done. How many books have you read that start out like gangbusters, only to lose their way in the middle, and then rush to a quick, disjointed ending (like the writer just wanted to get it over with)? Could be that's exactly what happened.

3. Read more. Many experienced writers will confide that good writing often reflects extensive reading. The books described in Chapter 3 are a great place to start, since they engage issues important to your aging parents in a style accessible to any age. See the box on page 118 for other examples of how to structure a children's book.

Whether in first or third person, the story should generally be told through the eyes of a single character – usually the main one. Narrate only what this chosen character would know and nothing he or she wouldn't: for example, other people's thoughts, or something out of sight. To switch to a different point of view, set up a separate section.

4. Characters

Some writers insist they need to know their characters thoroughly before they start writing. Others say they learn about their characters as they write – and sometimes are surprised in the process. Either way, characters come alive throughout the story, so your parents will want to make sure they know who these folks are that they're creating and what makes them tick, if only so they can keep them consistent. (The last thing a novice children's author wants to hear is some variation on, "But, Grandma, why in the world would they *do* something like that?")

The main character should be someone with whom the reader, in particular younger readers, can identify and/or sympathize. Often he or she will be near the top age of the intended readers. (One exception is in folktales.) It isn't necessary to provide a complete physical description or life's history. Rather, your parents can develop "character" through interesting details, such as a physical trait, a mannerism or quirk, or a favorite phrase.

Choosing names for their characters can be great fun. They can use names that have special meaning within the family, or they can avoid them to eliminate the appearance of playing favorites or inadvertently putting down an innocent relative. In children's books in particular, alliteration (repeating the first sounds in several adjacent words – Adam the Admirable Aardvark), rhyming (Amelia Bedelia and the legendary Cat in the Hat), silly puns and cockeyed characterizations add life and a sense of fun to the story.

Mystified by monikers? There's a whole website of naming ideas at groups.msn.com/WritingChildrensBooks/characternameslinks.msnw.

5. Setting

They should set their story in a place and time that is interesting to them or will be captivating to their readers. It can be real or fanciful, based on personal knowledge or derived from other sources, from a lifetime of reading to a few minutes of research.

Again, in a children's book, a little detail goes a long way. If the story is set in a castle, for example, a couple of pages on medieval architecture will be a snore. But a description of entering the secret twisty passage that leads to the mysterious chamber where the magic scrolls are supposed to be hidden will heighten suspense.

6. Style

Write simply and directly, in short words, short sentences, short paragraphs. Use dialog wherever possible, and be direct ("Go away!" instead of "He told her to go away.") As a simple rule of thumb, aim to tell at least one-third of the story through dialog.

Avoid big chunks of narration, especially description. If it's important, split it into smaller pieces, or convey it in dialog. For example, rather than describing a character with purple hair, let it come out through conversation: "I like your purple hair."

The tone should be positive and upbeat. They'll lose young readers in particular if the main character is downtrodden or full of attitude! And, for some novice writers at least, it may be necessary to walk a fine line between being warm and sweet, and being cutesy, maudlin or condescending.

A book, even a children's book, may seem like a lot for an aging parent to take on. But it can challenge, excite and rejuvenate, filling up hours that might otherwise drag. It's other-directed, so they're staying connected rather than turning in on themselves. It's something they can work on largely on their own – your involvement is as support and encourager, not ghostwriter (and least of all critic).

Best of all, there's a tangible outcome: a book that can be shown, shared and treasured for years.

End-Of-Life Issues

One of the expectations many readers have of a book is that, no matter how dire the subject or difficult the challenges, the author will somehow provide a happy ending. There's no disguising the realities of caregiving: Someday, the parents for whom you are providing care will be gone. Clearly, that's not a happy ending in the traditional sense. But it doesn't mean that their lives can't end well.

How you help them handle a number of end-of-life issues can play a major part in that. In this section, I'll look at your potential role in their quest for a renewed – or new – sense of spiritual direction. I'll return to the value of their stories, both in validating their lives and providing new depth and meaning to your own. And I'll take on the too-often tacky and emotional sides of the end of a life: figuring out who gets the stuff that's left behind.

Finally, in the concluding chapter of this book, I'll take a moment to reflect on the wide-ranging effects caregiving can and likely will have on the inner dynamics of your family, in particular (assuming you have one or more siblings) on the relationships you have with your brothers and sisters.

CHAPTER 13

Life Beyond Life:
The Quest For Spiritual Direction

I have walked with people at the end of their lives in my professional role as resident manager in senior-care communities, and in my personal life with my Mom and Grandpa Gus. Growing older and getting closer to their life's physical end causes many of our parents to reexamine their basic religious and spiritual beliefs. Some reconnect with them. Some reject them. And for others, the later stages of life inspire a quest for new meaning.

Whether they trust what's next or have many questions, deep down they're seeking comfort. And that can place unexpected stress on you as their caregiver. Few of us likely feel capable of providing spiritual direction to our parents at the end of their lives, let alone are we willing to assume that role.

The simplistic answer to the dilemma is "don't." Don't take on the role. Don't take on the stress. Don't take on the responsibility for guiding your parents to a spiritually peaceful and personally meaningful death. But don't run away from the issue, either. Recognize that as their life's horizon diminishes, their quest for timeless value may broaden, and be prepared to help them find those who can provide the guidance, the comfort and the sense of direction they seek.

The Spirit Is Willing

Oftentimes, I've been told by older adults that although their body is "falling apart," their spiritual connection is growing stronger and more all-encompassing. Even people with Alzheimer's disease sometimes seem to be connected on a spiritual level in a way we don't understand.

I remember working with a woman whose husband had mid-stage Alzheimer's. Her husband's brother died, and she struggled with whether to tell him, wondering if he'd understand. I agreed with her doctor that she should tell her husband, and added, "He probably already knows." Sure enough, the news of his brother's death wasn't news to him at all. On some level, in some way, he knew and had already moved on.

For people who have lived their lives in a material world, especially Boomers, deep spirituality can feel like new and uncharted territory. In *New Passages*, Gail Sheehy suggests that one of the goals during our parents' "second adulthood" is to gather all the elements of their lives and fit them into a personal creed – in essence, to figure out what they personally believe in and therefore act upon. Families can be brought together through their spiritual beliefs or torn apart by this process. In many ways, it depends on how we, as their adult children and caregivers, choose to handle it.

> *"Spiritual direction is, in reality, nothing more than a way*
> *of leading us to see and obey the real Director –*
> *the Holy Spirit hidden in the depths of our soul."*
> — Thomas Merton, Trappist monk

My Grandpa Gus came from a strong religious background. When he was dying, his sister called to ask me if anyone was addressing his spiritual needs. At that time, he was in a nursing home and, because he died in a small town, his pastor had been able to visit with him several times, so I knew he was receiving the support he wanted and could reassure his sister of that.

A few days before he died, he asked Eric to pray for him – he wanted more time. I asked him, "Grandpa, have you lived a good, full life?" to which he answered squarely, "Yes ma'am." He may not have been ready to leave this life, but I'm confident he wasn't concerned about where he was off to next.

Be aware that a number of diseases can affect your parents' ability to express their wishes about spirituality. My mother had Huntington's disease, a rare condition that causes parts of the brain to break down.

As her condition advanced, it was harder for her to express her wishes about many things.

For spiritual issues, my Dad, as her main caregiver, went by their history: Mom was Lutheran. End of discussion. She went to church on Sundays (well, except during Minnesota boating season, when you could listen to the church service on the radio while cruising down the Mississippi). Religion was her rock.

In the later years of her life, even though she couldn't directly tell my Dad that it was still important to her, when Sunday came there was no question whether or not they'd go to church. She dropped out of many other social venues, but not church. Church was the only place she wasn't embarrassed about being afflicted with Huntington's. She knew she wasn't fully in charge of herself, but also knew that her church family would accept her for who she was.

Defining Your Role

The key point here is one I've tried to make throughout this book: Our role as caregivers takes its cue from what our parents need from us, not what we can take hold of, either out of perceived need or a sense of responsibility (or guilt). The issue of spiritual direction can be an especially delicate one, since our belief systems may be very different from our parents' – and both will be refined in the crucible of their (and our own) increasingly limited mortality.

When you're caregiving, just sitting in silence with your parents sometimes brings the most peace. In some way, it connects you spiritually: They know you're there for them. After all, it's the quieter moments that give depth to our being and help us make sense of the world.

"Spiritual direction is the contemplative practice of
helping another person or group to awaken to
the mystery called God in all of life, and to
respond to that discovery in a growing relationship
of freedom and commitment."
— Father James Keegan, SJ

If you have the kind of relationship with your parents that makes it logical for you to raise spiritual issues, of course you should. One of Dick's sharpest memories is the day he spent with his dad pre-arranging funerals for his dad and mom. They worked out the clothes in which each would be buried. His dad spent a good half an hour picking out caskets to match. They worked out at which Catholic church the funeral Mass would be said. Who would pay for the organist and the flowers at the church. Even whether there should be a bugler at the cemetery to play "Taps," or just a recorded version. (Dick's dad and mom are both World War II veterans, so his dad opted for the real thing.)

Uncomfortable asking about your parents' spiritual beliefs straight out? Try a softer approach. Remember *Old Turtle* from Chapter 3? Old Turtle's explanation of God is open and accepting. It's a great resource from which to start or continue a conversation about spirituality.

If your parents are religious, you can cede this turf to those whose authority and credibility they accept. But think it through as you do. In many large congregations, regardless of the specific religion involved, personal attention is hard to come by. If your parents are seeking a greater level of time and attention than "their church" can provide, you might need to help them find a different, more intimate scale of spiritual support.

Finding Spiritual Direction

You have an increasingly sophisticated resource available to you in that regard: the "spiritual direction" movement. Though many of those involved in leadership roles are religiously trained, the object is not to proselytize for membership or allegiance, but rather to assist on a personal quest for meaning and direction.

According to Liz Budd Ellmann, Executive Director, Spiritual Directors International:

> *Spiritual direction explores a deeper relationship with the spiritual aspect of being human. Simply put, spiritual direction is helping people tell their sacred stories everyday. Spiritual direction has emerged in many contexts using language specific to particular cultural and spiritual traditions. Describing spiritual direction requires putting*

words to a process of fostering a transcendent experience that lies beyond all names and yet the experience longs to be articulated and made concrete in everyday living. It is easier to describe what spiritual direction does than what spiritual direction is. Spiritual direction helps us learn how to live in peace, with compassion, promoting justice, as humble servants of that which lies beyond all names.

Spiritual direction is not counseling, therapy or financial advice. There are many forms, but two major subsets can be found under this heading:

Formal spiritual direction involves a relationship with someone who has been trained as a spiritual director. Meetings can be one-on-one or in groups, and are generally held on a regular basis. There is a clear separation of roles between the guide and the person seeking the spiritual direction. Oftentimes, the spiritual director receives payment for services.

Informal spiritual companionship is characterized by a lack of structure and role definition. This type of spiritual direction is much more mutual. Meetings tend to happen spontaneously and are not regular. There is no exchange of fees and no one person who is the guide. As an example: regular walks with a friend with whom your parents can talk about spiritual issues.

Spiritual Directors International has a website that can help you learn more about the practice and find a spiritual director in your area (www.sdiworld.org).

> *"Randomness scares people.*
> *Religion is a way to explain randomness."*
> — Fran Lebowitz, author

The Monastic Model

At the annual meeting of the American Society on Aging several years ago, I attended a workshop on Benedictine spirituality. It was refreshing in that it did not deal directly with the topic of aging, but rather dealt with living in a model that leads to healthier aging.

Old age is, in a sense, a form of enforced monasticism in that it often involves a withdrawal from society. Like monasteries, where folks of similar spiritual belief gather, senior housing and senior centers gather up people of similar age. In exploring Benedictine spirituality here, I do not seek to persuade you to adopt The Rule of St. Benedict in a religious sense. I simply present it for your consideration – something to think about as you find yourself facing your parents' spiritual needs.

Monasteries are a part of most world religions and are known for housing people who practice a particular form of spiritual life. The Rule of St. Benedict is the basis for thousands of Christians who belong to the monastic movement.

Benedict of Nursia was born in Italy in 480. When he was a student in Rome, the empire was extremely prosperous, but morally corrupt. In the midst of all that, he decided that this kind of living did not represent the fullness of life. He left Rome for a rural setting in which to contemplate the meaning of life, simplify its demands, and refashion his own attitudes and lifestyle.

> *"The object of spiritual direction is to cultivate one's*
> *ability to discern God's presence in one's life –*
> *to notice and appreciate moments of holiness,*
> *to maintain an awareness of the interconnectedness*
> *of all things, to explore ways to be open*
> *to the Blessed Holy One in challenging*
> *and difficult moments as well as in joyful ones."*
> — Rabbi Jacob Staub

What he created reflected balance and good healthy practice. The Rule of St. Benedict teaches basic monastic virtues: humility, silence, obedience and directions for daily living. It suggests times for common prayer, meditation, reading of sacred scripture and manual labor.

The difference between the Rule of St. Benedict and other monastic guidelines is that he recommended moderation. Limits were imposed for fasting and all-night prayer in order to maintain health. He recommended working with the hands (manual labor) six hours a day, but also having leisure time for reading and common prayer. His recipe for prayer, fasting and service ensures the values expressed in the Bible are lived in a balanced way.

One of the best experiences I had teaching Elderhostels was at a monastery in northwestern Minnesota. I grew up Lutheran, closed-minded to other religions, and ignorant as well. Happily, working with the nuns, and observing and taking part in their practice, opened my mind and heart to a different way to experience spirituality.

"The destination of all is to God."
— Surah 35:18

Benedictine spirituality strives for a balance of spending time with yourself and with God while being an active member of a community. Retirement or older age is one of the times in your parents' lifespan where society gives the okay for them to be contemplative. It is acceptable to sit and just "be." The Rule of St. Benedict may provide a practical model for that, regardless of their individual allegiance.

Application For Today

Being spiritual doesn't just mean attending services at a church, or synagogue, or mosque, or temple. Rather, it means paying attention and tuning in to forge a personally meaningful connection with God as a routine part of life – whatever your parents conceive God to be, and by whatever name they describe this presence (or absence).

To me, it's not a matter of who's right and who's not, but more a matter of appreciating all practices that can bring peace and comfort to your parents in their later years. The first step is to be open to *their* desires, and willing to learn if that's what *they* need you to do.

For most of us in our working and parenting lives, running like chickens with our heads cut off is the only way of living we know. We praise busyness and condemn being still. Through exploring the Rule of St. Benedict, I have been able to better understand the importance of sitting still through prayer and meditation, while remaining a productive player in society.

There is – or should be, I believe – a wonderful sense of peace with death. In my experience, hospice care in particular has a touching way of helping many families experience that peace. A key part of feeling it, however, is knowing you did the best you could – both as a caregiver and as a daughter or son.

Our parents are going to die. We can't stop that from happening, however much we may want to. But it's important that we don't run away from the reality. Our parents need us to experience as much of this end-of-life process with them as we can. To the extent that we are willing and able to do so, we can provide care that supports both them and ourselves.

In turn, the lessons we learn will become a part of our own approach to the later stages of life.

> *"Buddhist practioners may meditate, learn from teachers,*
> *chant, or pray. Through learning from a dharma teacher*
> *(at a retreat or otherwise), one can explore*
> *and apply direction toward a spiritual life*
> *that is less theoretical, and more personal.*
> *With spiritual friends, one can find ongoing*
> *support for the spiritual lifestyle*
> *one has chosen to live."*
> — Pamela Ayo Yetunde, hospital chaplain

When Death Comes

Mary Oliver says a great deal about spirituality and the end of life in her poem, "When Death Comes." At the end of my life, I want her words (only part of her eloquence is quoted here) to speak for me:

> When it's over, I want to say: all my life
> I was a bride married to amazement.
> I was a bridegroom, taking the world into my arms.
>
> When it's over, I don't want to wonder
> if I have made of my life something particular, and real.
> I don't want to find myself sighing and frightened,
> or full of argument.
>
> I don't want to end up simply having visited this world.

CHAPTER 14

Lives That Keep On Living: Preserving Family Stories

I remember sitting at my sister's kitchen table with my Grandma Gladys. I had brought along a tape recorder and asked if she would re-tell stories she had told me through the years.

"Why do you want to record these stories?" she asked.

"So I don't forget – and so others can hear about your wild adventures," I told her.

If you knew my grandmother in her later years, you'd never suspect that she'd had a wild side. As I was growing up, Grandma Gladys never seemed to want to plan anything because she might get a headache. But as the tape recorder ran on, I discovered there was so much more to her.

For one thing, she'd engaged in "illegal activities." In her day, it was against the policy of many businesses for married women to work. She liked her job at the bank so much, she lied about being married to keep it. She finally had to quit when she got pregnant with my Mom.

When she was going with Grandpa Floyd, they used to take the overnight train from Minneapolis to Chicago with another couple to go dancing all Saturday night. They'd return late Sunday and stumble into work Monday morning with very little sleep, but wonderful memories.

Grandma Gladys had had a wild spirit. We didn't often see it in her later years. But we heard it through her stories. As she told me of daring adventures, and taking risks, and the joy that came from those times, her face lit up. In her stories, she was still full of life and energy – not the grandma we had come to know.

What a gift to pass on to me. I saw a different side of her and learned the value of taking risks and having fun in life.

Memories You Want

Like Grandma Gladys, our parents will die. Before they do, we have an opportunity to preserve their voices, and their values, through the stories they can tell us. We've talked about storytelling in our discussions of scrapbooking (Chapter 8) and writing a children's book (Chapter 12), but more in the context of how to do it. We've also touched on the idea briefly in other places. At the risk of belaboring the subject, I'd like to return to storytelling – and story preserving – one more time. But this time, in the context of what's in it for us, both as caregivers and as our parents' children.

I can't count the times I've talked to someone struggling with providing care to an aging parent and heard a common lament: "There's just nothing for us to talk about." Idle chit-chat only takes you so far. The tough issues are often hard to dig into. In between, there doesn't seem to be anything to fill the hours constructively.

Capturing and preserving stories can provide those gap-fillers. Stories engage both the teller and the listener, awakening old memories and creating new ones. They reveal the values and beliefs that have permeated our parents' lives, and very likely conditioned our own. They open the door to more substantive conversations.

And they give us one last chance to hang onto pieces of our family heritage – pieces that very possibly will be lost forever when our parents die. If you're at all interested in retracing family roots, your parents' stories can contribute rich and wide-ranging details, adding more personal dimensions to the basics of genealogy even as they provide clues of new places to look.

Don't fight your parents when they launch into yet another telling of a familiar story. Don't check your watch, hoping to discover you have someplace else to go. Think selfishly: There's something here for you. Encourage your parents to revisit the stories that occupy swatches of the canvas of their lives. Better yet, work with them to preserve those stories. The result can be a priceless resource that you'll find deeply rewarding for years to come – compensation for the time and energy you're devoting now as a caregiver.

Putting Things In Writing

There are two basic mediums available to you in preserving what are increasingly being called "life stories": writing and recording. For our generation, as well as our parents', the former will be more familiar – but the latter may feel (and be) less like work.

Many of the writing tips and tactics we've discussed in other places apply here as well, including journaling. To assist and simplify this form of writing, you'll find many stores now carry "memory journals": handy books, mostly with blank lined pages, organized into topics or with fill-in-the-blank questions.

Software packages also are available, and the Internet, of course, is a growing resource. As a sample of what's online, you can visit LifeBio (www.lifebio.com), which offers such things as a template with 250 questions designed to help someone build their own autobiography. Your Life Is Your Story (www.your-life-your-story.com) also features a variety of tools and techniques.

If you prefer to make things up as you go, a simple way to start is by creating a timeline to serve as an outline and framework. Your parents can pinpoint significant events on the timeline, then move deeper to notes about things both significant and insignificant. As with brainstorming, this is a process where quantity typically is more important than quality. Be a packrat while you're in collection mode. Edit and arrange later.

Another way to go is to develop your own list as a starting point: Stories you want to hear again in order to preserve them, people you want to know more about, blanks in your family story, especially your parents' lives, that only your parents can fill in.

If they're initially reluctant, don't overwhelm them with an open-ended quest to pry into every memory nook and cranny. Instead of concentrating on their entire life, start with a smaller piece to digest: a particular period or event. From a couple of smaller stories, some patterns may emerge that can help organize a larger narrative. And you'll all become more comfortable with the process.

For some parents, telling their story in the first person – "I did this; I thought that" – will be a little awkward. In those cases, a useful trick is to encourage them to write or narrate as if they were detailing someone else's life. Referring to themselves in the third person might take a little getting used to, but if it helps dampen some of their conflicting emotions, or relieves self-consciousness about "bragging" or "telling tales," it will help them stay focused on the story itself.

Once finished, the collection of their life stories can take any number of final forms: a completed store-bought journal or diary; a scrapbook; a collection of pictures with captions; a conventional book. To take the collection to another level entirely, augment stories with favorite poems and music, memorabilia, and reprinted information from conventional sources (newspapers, magazines, etc.).

A Recorded Record

If the idea of writing is daunting, or seems too time-consuming, recording might be the more comfortable alternative: Have your parents talk their life stories into a tape recorder, or set up the family video camera and create your own oral history.

Dick has been doing this with his dad, a prolific storyteller whose eye for detail hasn't dimmed in his 90s. It's a bittersweet process for them because of the constant reminder that they started too late to balance his dad's memories with his mom's, who descended into a non-Alzheimer's dementia a number of years ago. Moral of the story: Don't wait to start – you don't know how much time you have.

Here are a few tips from Dick's personal oral history project (plus his experience as a television reporter and independent video producer).

Put the camera to the side: Even though his digital video camera is relatively small, it's an imposing presence sitting parked on a tripod in his dad's line of sight. He sets it up a little off to one side, then leaves the camera and sits closer to his dad, just out of the camera shot, to provide a focal point. It's much easier to tell a story to some*one* than some*thing*.

Leave the shot alone: A happy byproduct of not standing behind the camera is relief from the temptation to constantly fiddle with it, zooming in, pulling back, and perhaps breaking rapport with the storyteller. Lock on a medium shot – close enough to see your subject's facial expressions, far enough away that they won't inadvertently move out of the frame – then leave it be.

Get good sound: Built-in microphones on cameras are notoriously poor. What's worse, they're omni-directional: They'll pick up sound

Hey, Mom And Dad, Tell Me About ...

Books you've enjoyed
Building something
Cartoon favorites
Child-raising stories
Christmas stories
Close-call stories
Cold War stories
Courtship stories
Difficulty stories
Dream stories
Entrepreneurial stories
Escape stories
Family stories (past generations)
Farm stories
Favorite places
Food stories
Happy stories

Hard times
Immigration stories
Meeting each other
Miracle stories
Music that moved you
Neighbor stories
Pet/animal stories
Picnic stories
Prank stories
Religious/Spiritual stories
School stories
Sports stories
Standing firm stories
Train stories
Trespassing stories
UFO stories
War stories
Work stories

from anywhere around them. The closer to the storyteller you can put the sound-recording device, the better. Even basic video cameras have plug-ins for microphone peripherals that greatly improve the audio quality of what your storyteller is telling you. Best choice: a lavaliere (tie-tack) that can be unobtrusively clipped to a shirt or blouse.

Minimize distractions: Turn off the phone. Get away from the kids, the TV, the dog and anything else that might interrupt a good story at a crucial moment. Dick likes to interview one-on-one; if more than one other person is around, he finds it becomes both a distraction and an inhibiting presence.

Minimize movement: If you put someone in a rocking chair, they'll rock. If they're sitting in a chair that squeaks, you just know it's going to make enough noise to drive you nuts. Get your subject settled and comfortable, but try to avoid reasons for them to jump up and fetch something. If they need a prop, or will want to refer to something later, have it nearby from the beginning. Or go get it yourself.

Keep the sessions short: The videotapes Dick uses come in 60- and 80-minute lengths. He uses 60s with his dad, and that's an outer limit. An hour is a long time for someone to be "on" – even if they're revisiting familiar ground. Watch for signs of fatigue, including impatience and cutting a story short that you know could run longer. Better several shorter sessions than a long one where your subject runs out of energy and enthusiasm.

Talk little, listen much: Storytellers love to tell their stories, and it usually takes very little prompting to get them going. Once they're off and running, let 'em go. Others may be a little more inhibited by the camera's presence. For them, start with a few easy questions so they get comfortable before trying to lead into something heavier or more involved. If they wander off on a tangent, let them finish their thought before gently bringing them back to where they got off-track. Or explore the tangent in greater detail. Who knows where that will go?

Keep tapes clean and labeled: Label your oral history tapes immediately with who and when – an unlabeled tape looks too available. Put tapes in a safe, dry, out-of-the-way place where no one will be tempted to use them to record a Simpson's rerun. Even after you've pulled out segments to use in some kind of edited program, keep them for later review. Every time you look at your "raw footage," you'll see and hear something new.

Be Systematic

Whether you're writing or using tape, adjust your role to make sure something is accomplished: interviewer, compiler, fact-checker, editor. You may want to set up a regular schedule for storytelling to keep yourself and your parents on track. Without making the process a burden – for either of you – a schedule, however flexible, provides a place and a pace for staying organized and making progress.

In between sessions, you can be thinking about new questions and your parents can be sorting through additional materials or making notes on their own. If they're comfortable with a tape recorder, have them keep one at hand and make voice notes when they think of something.

Beyond basic conversation, almost any stimulus can trigger a story or memory: Pictures, knickknacks around the house, old clothes in a closet, the aroma of food cooking or leaves burning, a song or the voice of an icon from their past (Walter Cronkite, Johnny Carson, the Andrews Sisters). If the prospect of hearing the same old stories again and again isn't at all attractive, ask for new ones. Need some suggestions? Use the list on page 140.

Be aware that systematically mining memories for life stories can dredge up some deep emotions. In *Share Your Life Story: New Writing Approach for Elders*, posted on the website of the American Society on Aging (www.asaging.org), Kate de Medeiros and Thomas R. Cole present a process called "re-stor(y)ing" your life and warn:

> *"Unearthing the treasures by re-stor(y)ing lives does not come easily. Sadness, fear, anxiety and resistance impede the creative process of excavation. Vulnerability is inevitable as people searching for their buried pasts through writing have two forces to confront: their own reactions to their pasts and the reactions of perceived readers to their works."*

In our younger years, many of us struggled to find meaning in and for our lives. Many older adults face a similar struggle today. Remembering their trials and hardships, as well as their achievements and blessings, can yield deep insights in this regard.

That's yet another reason to help your parents tell their stories at this stage of life. In the process of passing valuable lessons on to others, they may find new and needed pride in themselves. As they do so, they will rediscover the core values and beliefs they hold dear.

It may be very difficult for your parents to dig up memories from their past. It also may be painful. Know this, and be prepared to support them in the event they need additional help. By establishing a safe place, and reassuring them when they falter, you can help them experience both a sense of personal achievement (in finishing the task) and family approval (for helping others better understand and appreciate their heritage).

Listening From The Heart

One of the greatest things you can do for your parents is listen to their stories – even if you've heard them a hundred times before. In their stories, your parents find a safe and nurturing place where they are heard and feel validated. Simply by telling their stories, they can share the wisdom and experience they've accumulated. Simply by asking, even when you know full well what you might hear, you're telling them their lives are still important to you.

If anything, now's the time to pay even more attention. In the process of their storytelling, your parents may give you important insights into both their mental and physical health. Do the stories they tell focus on positives or negatives? Are the details still sharp and clear, or are they fading – or changed? Has the tone or emphasis shifted? Does their choice of stories, or the way they tell a familiar tale, give you a clue to things they may be reluctant to come right out and say – but really want to find a way to talk with you about?

Many people don't realize how much they have accomplished or learned until they deliberately and systematically set the events of a lifetime down for the next generation. And many of their adult children will be amazed to discover new and unsuspected dimensions in their parents.

As Anne Frank wrote in *The Diary of a Young Girl*: "I want to write, but more than that, I want to bring out all kinds of things that lie buried in my heart." What a wonderful gift to help your parents give you.

CHAPTER 15

Who Gets The Stuff:
Don't Let The Possessions
Come To Own You

I remember peeking in the china cabinet before my Mom died in 2002, checking out what she had for dishes and collectables that I would possibly want. What I found were Post-It notes on various items, identifying in Mom's handwriting who should get what – or at least who she wanted to receive a specific item.

I never talked about it, either one-on-one with Mom or with my family. My sister Anne and I were the only ones who knew about the notes. It would have been very easy for us to make changes to our benefit, with no one the wiser. It also would have been very simple to bring up the notes in conversation with Steve and Dave, our brothers, at a family gathering. ("Mom's been trying to decide who gets what of her stuff – is there anything you really want that she should know about?") We did neither.

In that, I suspect we're normal. Why don't we talk about an issue as basic as who mom and dad would prefer to get their stuff when they die? According to Marlene S. Stum, Ph.D. (Family Social Science) at the University of Minnesota:

> *"Denial of our own or other's mortality is often at the [heart of] why conversations about inheritance can be so sensitive. Few family members want to give the impression that a family member might die or that they would want someone to die. Talking about human losses or changes in health can be both emotional and filled with legal and financial complexities many find overwhelming. In some cases, a*

family history of conflict among parents, in-laws, and siblings will influence if and how family members can communicate about later life transitions of aging parents."

The Process Of Passing On

Nothing I've seen suggests there's a norm for how families handle the issue of who gets mom and dad's stuff. Sometimes, the parents decide on their own. Sometimes, I'm sure, it's done collaboratively. Mostly, I'd be willing to guess, the kids have to figure it out as a part of settling the estate. I've certainly seen that scenario far more often than any other alternative.

It's understandable: We don't talk about passing on possessions because it's too close to talking about our parents passing on, and death is a subject our culture mostly avoids at any cost. That's too bad, because end-of-life planning is such an important thing to do, and divvying up the stuff – in a way that's meaningful and satisfying to your parents – should be part of that process.

Don't look on it as morbid. If anything, as a matter of practicality, it will be easier to make decisions before a triggering event (like death) occurs. There's time for your parents to choose how they want the process handled. There's time to let everyone in the family be as involved or uninvolved as they want to be. There's time to make decisions, and then make changes to those decisions.

Trust me: You don't want to put this off until your parents are gone and you're selling the house and disposing of the stuff that's still in it in a mad rush to settle the estate. Emotions are going to be too raw at that point. This really should be a joyous event.

After all, possessions are just things. In the larger scheme of life, things are not as important as the love and time we share with each other in our families. Yet decisions about personal belongings – sometimes referred to legally as "non-titled property" – often turn out to be more challenging and emotion-laden than decisions about titled property (like houses and cars) or the financial wealth accumulated over a lifetime.

Yes, families fight over money. But sometimes the fights over "stuff" are the really nasty ones. Those are the ones where the battle lines are drawn over intangible forms of value – sentimental rather than strictly financial, and sometimes spanning several generations – that the years have infused into the otherwise innocent and ordinary possessions that help define a lifetime.

What to do? *Who Gets Grandma's Yellow Pie Plate?* is a wonderful resource for adult children and parents to use in discussing the passing on of personal possessions. It's a practical, large-print, 95-page workbook put out by the University of Minnesota Extension Service (www.extension.umn.edu/info-u/finances/BF840.html). It includes nine different worksheets designed to identify and decide what to do with things that don't have a legal title that clarifies ownership, but may have real value in the context of a family. It even has a separate video that explains the process envisioned. It not only guides in passing on the possessions themselves, but also helps take inventory of emotions along the way.

Who Should Choose

Although there's no established norm, I've seen two approaches if you're prepared to engage this issue before you absolutely have to. It comes down to whose decisions drive the process, your parents' or their children's.

Nothing says your parents have to carry this load. Lists are always a good place to start, and mom and dad do not have to make them. Rather, they can encourage their children (and perhaps also their grandchildren) to identify those items that are meaningful to them. If only one person wants something, issue solved. If there are conflicts, at least now they're visible and there's a starting point for working toward a solution that, with luck and a little understanding, will appear fair to all.

The value of having children identify the items they want, and sharing why, extends far beyond avoiding fights. It's also a wonderful way for your parents to see the emotional connections their family members have with their stuff – and consequently their lives. Those are memories well worth sharing.

For example, because we live with my Dad, we have access to a distinctive green cookie jar. (Since my Dad's still alive, he still has most of Mom's stuff.) It's old. It's ugly. But it's exactly the kind of thing that could someday cause great conflict, not because it's worth anything, but because it was the cookie jar that my Mom always filled with homemade goodies.

It was kept in a lower cupboard, providing easy access for kids grabbing a handful as they passed through the kitchen. The trick was not to let Mom know you were in there. My brother Steve practiced opening and closing that jar so as not to be heard. Of his many visits, some were foiled by Mom's voice from the other room saying, "Get out of the cookies, you'll spoil your dinner." But many others succeeded.

Who gets that cookie jar? Someday, Steve. To the rest of us, it's just something ugly and green that we remember – however fondly – from our childhoods. To Steve, it's something special.

Taking Chances

If no one in your family is inclined to be a decision maker and risk making waves, try the lottery technique. I've worked with many families that have opted for this alternative. If you're working from people's lists, and an item is desired by more than one person, you draw lots. If there's no list or advance distribution system, when the time comes to go through mom and dad's possessions, each sibling pulls a number out of a hat and gets to choose one item at a time. (It may feel fairer to go through the order first to last, then last to first.)

This way, your parents can remove themselves from the deciding role, and any suggestion that their decisions reflect value judgments about who is loved the most. For this to work, though, everyone has to let go of the outcome and be okay with "the luck of the draw."

Depending on the size and closeness of your family, you may want to set up a special time to do this together, like a holiday gathering. You may also decide that the last thing you want to risk is trashing a holiday squabbling about stuff. In that case, handle this over time, perhaps from a distance.

Whichever, it's worth doing sooner rather than later. I once had a discussion with a friend over lunch about this issue. He ventured that it's not on the parents to distribute their possessions. Rather, as he put it, "Let the kids duke it out after they're gone."

How unfair for the children. And the parents! Emotions run deep after a death, and I believe knowingly providing the fuel for a flash fire can only cause hardship – for everybody. Better, I contend, to take the situation in hand while there's time to plan, and amend plans. That way, the kids are involved and at least understand the process. Best case, everybody is happy with the outcome, which means mom and dad can be happy about it, too.

And If Nobody Cares?

What about the stuff nobody wants? For your parents, it can be difficult to discover that no one in the family cares about things they certainly consider of value. In every community, however, there are organizations both public and private that work with those who have little and need much. Your parents may not have the joy of knowing that the things they value will be enjoyed by someone in the family. But they can take some satisfaction in knowing their stuff won't simply be tossed – that it will "go to a good home."

It's more likely that some of their kids will revert to childhood and perhaps care a little too much, which can lead to conflict that's painful not just for the participants, but for your parents as well. After my Mom died, my sister Anne and I spent way too much time arguing over who would get her diamond rings. There were three of them, a set, and Mom hadn't decided. As her mother did before her, she let us fight over them instead. Not a nice thing to do.

We exchanged some nasty comments, dug up old family dirt, pushed each other's emotional buttons – the usual. Predictably, my brothers accepted the fact that they were out of the running. (Although, come to think of it, who declared that boys can't inherit diamond rings?)

It was too soon after Mom died. The rings had meaning to each of us, but they also brought up old stuff. That's what possessions do: Provide a stimulus that brings to the surface buried feelings about the relationships we've had with our parents and our siblings through the years – everything from who did how much when to which one really was the favorite daughter.

Because my sister and I couldn't decide, Mom's rings went into Dad's safe-deposit box. And there they stayed for a full year, until I suggested he make a decision about them before he married for the second time. "Do whatever you want with the rings," I told him.

What Have They Got?

Even if your parents have downsized their lifestyle through the years, you might be amazed by how much "stuff" they have – and how many different ways there are to decide what becomes of it. Furniture and appliances are obvious, of course, as are collectables: art, antiques, jewelry and all the other things people today choose to make a point of hanging onto. Pets we discussed in Chapter 6, but there's also:

Kitchenware – both the everyday stuff and perhaps a set of good china and silverware.

Linens – tablecloths, sheets and towels, quilts and comforters, needlework, crafts, plus "family" clothes with special meaning (baptismal gowns, wedding dresses, military and sports uniforms, and the like).

Pictures and documents – not just snapshots (whether in albums or boxes), but old movies, correspondence, diaries and journals, and legal papers (their wedding license, degrees and diplomas, military papers, etc.).

Decorations and knickknacks – for both inside and outside.

Tools – in the workshop and in the garage.

Sports and recreational gear – including guns and fishing tackle as well as toys and athletic equipment.

Books, records, musical instruments, trophies, keepsakes, and all the other assorted flotsam and jetsam of long and busy lives.

"Give them to one of us kids, cash them in, give them away. But you make a decision. Don't leave it for us."

That year I turned 40, and Dad presented me with a little box. I was caught flat-footed. "He's giving me a part of the three-ring set," I thought to myself. "He's made a new ring. He's given me the wedding band."

I never thought he'd present me with the entire three-ring set, but that's what he did. With a twist, however. When I immediately asked, "What about Anne," he said, "I want you to wear the rings as they are, not break up the set. On Kristi's 40th birthday (Kristi is Anne's only daughter and my Dad's only biological granddaughter), I want you to give the rings to Kristi. She can do whatever she wishes with them. So, in a sense, you're the keeper of the rings."

As Solomon-like solutions go, I thought it was pretty good. Anne, on the other hand, was not happy. After a year of not talking to me, however, we met at our favorite restaurant and she said, "This is

With This Ring

At my Grandma Jo's funeral in 1994, my paternal grandfather, Grandpa Gus, gave my sister Anne grandma's wedding ring. Anne was the oldest granddaughter, and she and Grandma Jo had a close relationship. I know it was very special for Anne to have Grandpa Gus give her that ring. She wears it to this day.

Grandma Gladys, my maternal grandmother, was still living. When she heard what happened, she took off her thin wedding band and gave it to me. "Here Kari," she said, "since Anne got Grandma Jo's ring, I'd like you to have mine."

It was incredibly special for her to give me her ring while she was alive. She knew I had admired that small band ever since I was little. I wear it along with my wedding bands and consider it a priceless heirloom.

stupid to be fighting over rings. I was mad. I don't want to be mad anymore. I want to be with my sister."

I love to wear Mom's rings. But I don't wear them around Anne. It was a tremendous gift to me, but an element of guilt still accompanies it. Meanwhile, Kristi turns 40 in 2024. I know it will hurt to pass the rings on at that time. But I'll do it.

Do It Now!

Whatever they leave and to whomever they leave it, it's important to help your parents think about the action of giving: They have the right to give as they wish, but they need to know that their actions will affect both those to whom they give things and those who aren't included. Their giving can be narcissistic or selfless, inspiring or vindictive – and sometimes the line between is faintly drawn at best. (In some families, in fact, parents choose to skip a generation entirely, gifting their grandchildren instead of their children, just to avoid the turmoil.)

As a culture, we put too much emphasis on stuff. Now, in your parents' later years, that can come back to create new heartaches – and headaches – for the family. Don't let the things in your parents' lives become a source of anguish and argument in yours. Help them decide quickly and simply, and then move on to more important concerns.

CHAPTER 16

Family Caregiving: What Are You Getting Yourself Into?

I have always had crazy relationships with my sister and two brothers, sometimes loving, sometimes tense. When we get together, however, we laugh. Even in hard times, we find the humor.

When we were taking care of Grandpa Gus, Steve and Dave came home to Minnesota (from Colorado and New Hampshire respectively) to see him before he died. Grandpa Gus had a lot of slides, and after dinner we'd set up the projector and view old family pictures together: my three siblings, assorted cousins, in-laws, an aunt, Dad. We saw those embarrassing pictures you hope have been lost – you know, the one of you in the bathtub as a kid, the high school awkward prom date, the ridiculous hairdo and glasses.

The slide that cracked us all up was the one of Dave, at about age 3, dolled up in a cute pink dress, blush on his cheeks and grinning like a fool. We all laughed until our sides split. I had a print made of that one, put it in a pretty pink frame, and sent it to his girlfriend. According to brother Dave, that picture is still in a drawer. His girl-friend is "allowed" to take it out occasionally – but she's not encour-aged to do so too often.

The point is, I'm fortunate with my siblings. We've been through the fires of family caregiving together, and come out of it closer and stronger for it, and able to laugh about it. You may or may not have had the same good fortune with your brothers and sisters up to now. No matter: providing care to your parents in the years to come is going to test those bonds.

Ready Or Not

I work as a caregiver coach to a number of Baby Boomers with aging parents. Generally, the ones who call me are very much like me: They're the ones who take on the family issues. From experience, I know this isn't always a welcomed role, but it is one they feel fits them somehow. One of the things I do is show them all the various pieces that might become a part of their family's unique situation so they can see what they're getting into and enlist help from their siblings from the beginning.

To bring everyone closer and help to define those roles at the onset of a crisis, or at a trigger point, I recommend a family meeting. I've been involved in several such meetings, including one with my own family when my Grandpa Gus needed care. I opened the meeting by having us go around the table and check in. After each person was able to express feelings, we made sure everyone was clear about grandpa's diagnosis and what he needed for care. We then allocated the tasks among us. Even though the tasks didn't end up being accomplished exactly as assigned, it helped to have everybody aware of how much needed to be done.

Here are some of those basic roles you and your siblings may be called upon to fill. Use them as a guide when you're talking about who will do what.

Helping with activities of daily living: Professionals refer to them as ADLs: the essentials of getting by on a day-to-day basis. Among them are core activities like bathing and toileting that very little in your life may have prepared you to take over. Are you ready to see your parents naked? Helpless? Wipe their butts for them? Clean up after them? And are your parents ready for that kind of care – when you're the one providing it? In some families, this comes naturally. For most, it's equally difficult on the parents and their adult children.

Ringing the immediate realities like ripples spreading around a rock dropped in a pond are others. Is your parents' home set up to make it easier for someone to come in and help them? Can you rearrange it so they can continue to live in it, or is a move to some other form of housing going to be necessary – if not immediately, in the foreseeable future? Are there issues of arthritis to deal with? Disruptive behavior from dementia? Pain? With time and a little basic training, some of the anxiety common to new situations will pass. But expect a period of adjustment for both you and your parents if you start to take on these intimate responsibilities.

Helping with instrumental activities of daily living: Professionals call these IADLs. If your parents can no longer drive, and transportation isn't readily available or accessible, will you be providing taxi service? Who will do their shopping? Cook their meals? How about cleaning? Doctor appointments can be a drawn-out affair and take up most of your day. Do you have to be there? And how about spending time with and keeping them occupied?

In contrast to ADLs, which typically have to be done right away, these peripheral activities often will cause more tension and strain. From your point of view, they don't absolutely have to be done right this minute. From your parents' vantage point, sooner is better than later. Here's where the balancing act gets complicated as you try to handle the needs of your own family, career and other responsibilities – which, of course, have not gone away – along with a new, and sometimes unpredictable, workload. If you're not getting support from your sibs (or if you've pushed them away and taken on more than you might have needed to), balance is even harder to come by.

Managing paid homecare workers: Yes, you can hire folks to help with your parents' care, from physical therapy and companionship to cleaning and cooking. But outsiders brought into your parents' home also represent a managerial responsibility for someone: hiring, perhaps firing, paying, replacing, supervising, scheduling – the list goes on and on.

Besides finding competent and caring (not to mention honest) workers, someone needs to teach them about your folks' likes and dislikes, explain their needs and behaviors, orient them to their changing needs. Someone also may need to step in and referee conflicts when your parents aren't happy with what's being done for them, or by whom. Some workers will just click; others will struggle. And one day, one of them will not show up. Then what? What's your backup plan? (Figure that your parents will call you first and expect you to pick up the slack.)

Battling the healthcare system: For a trained professional, trying to make things happen in our country's cumbersome system of public, private and personal providers is a daunting challenge. For you, it can be all but overwhelming. In our medical care system, fragmentation is the order of the day. Your parents' physician will not always be available or aware of their day-to-day needs or wishes – with many HMOs, they may not see the same physician on a regular basis. More often, you may talk to office assistants or a nurse, none of whom will necessarily have been kept in the loop, and none of whom may have the ability to actually do anything on your parents' behalf.

Whoever takes on this particular role needs to be an assertive communicator. As their care-requiring conditions advance, you may not be able to depend on your parents to make sense of the medical advice they're receiving. You'll increasingly need to be in the room with them: to hear what they're telling their doctors (which may not be anything at all like what they're telling you), to hear what their doctors are telling them (much of which they won't remember without you reminding them), and in particular to ask questions that otherwise probably won't be asked – questions that may help head off problems or better control manageable conditions, provided the proper preventative steps are taken.

Supervising in the face of dementia: Helping with any of the above becomes much more complicated when you factor in a frightened or hostile or disoriented parent. Even without dementia, many people don't adjust well to illness, at any age. With dementia complicating the situation, the frustration is magnified. You're trying to cope with someone to whom the plea "be reasonable" may have little meaning or relevance – someone who, in your memories, is still a warm and competent individual. Now, their feelings can come out in anger and frustration seemingly aimed right at you. Yet another can of worms. Anyone who takes care of a parent with dementia needs to be flexible, patient and empathetic – and a sense of humor helps a lot.

Finding Family Balance

It's impossible to cover every variation on sibling and family relationships, or cross-match them to every conceivable caregiver role someone in the family may be asked to play. In your communications with your siblings, focus on being as clear as possible about the care your parents need and want, not on everybody else's baggage. Some of your siblings may surprise you with their willingness to jump in and lend a hand, while others will disappoint you by doing everything but running away from the new realities of your parents' lives.

Understand that each of you has had an individual relationship with your parents, just as each of you now has a life beyond the old family structure. You all need to respect each other for both. Don't forget spouses and other family members. Keep them included, if they wish to be, but also remember that they, too, need time to adjust to the realities of caregiving.

I remember facilitating a family caregiving meeting for five adult children and a number of support people. The primary caregiver was tired and wanted her siblings to understand that, by keeping their father on life support, they were not only going against his wishes, but also extending her role to the point of exhaustion. When two of her siblings said that she didn't need to be at the hospital all the time, she was furious. "Who's going to catch the mistakes?" she raged. "Who's going to hold dad's hand? Who's going to catch the doctor when he comes by if I'm not there?"

Her need was to be heard and understood, especially when she felt the rest of the family was going against their father's final wishes. But her siblings needed her to understand that while she had taken on the primary role, it wasn't an exclusive one. Just as she needed to be there, they also needed to be able to help out and be involved in their own unique ways.

It's worth noting that even if you're prepared to play the primary role, it may not always be what's needed. I could not have taken care of my mother full-time. My Dad was her caregiver – my role was supporting Dad. And I wasn't the only one of their children involved.

When my Mom was in the hospital with what she and Dad first thought was "a bad case of the flu," the doctors wanted to perform a colonoscopy to help them in their diagnosis. This meant, of course, that Mom had to drink that horrible antifreeze-like fluid. And lots of it.

Mom had this rather desperate look on her face when Anne and I arrived. "I can't drink this," she said. "I just can't." I had no idea what to do, but Anne plunked herself down by Mom and poured her a big cup of the yellow liquid. "Oh, yes, you can," she said cheerfully. "Here we go ... drink up."

Hard Questions

 As your parents grow older, expect the need for tough decisions to keep coming.

Should you sit in on their doctor's appointments to make sure your parents are accurately describing how they feel and what they need? Whether they want you to or not? Should you call ahead before the appointment to prime the doctor with things your parents may not bring up?

If you think your parents are depressed, should you ask their doctor to put them on medication?

When you begin to notice that your parents can't keep up with the house, or that their own hygiene is suffering, how intrusive do you become in areas such as cleaning, bathing, cooking and the like?

As their driving abilities decline, at what point should you mention the idea of giving up the car keys? And when they're unable or unwilling to face reality, are you going to be prepared to take them away?

When you think it's time for your parents to move to a more institutional form of housing, how do you raise the subject? How hard do you lobby for one community vs. another? If they're not prepared to put their names on a waiting list, should you do it anyway?

I can't give you simple, hard-and-fast answers to questions like these. When I coach adult children of seniors, I advise them to make a decision based on their relationship with their parents and the consensus (or lack thereof) among their siblings. The more you know about your parents' situation, the better equipped you'll be to help them determine a course of action – or take hold of the decision-making process yourself as conditions warrant.

By golly, Mom finished on time and away she went for her proce-
dure. If I'm ever in the hospital, you'd better believe Anne is the one
I'll want by my bed, reading magazines, watching TV, sorting my
mail, helping with meals. It's her role, one that fits her, and one she
handles very capably. While I'm off finding the nurses and doctors,
talking about what's next, calling in-home nursing care, and updating
other members of the family, Anne is the one who can be totally
present and supportive at the bedside.

Expect The Unexpected

Distance presents a terrible dilemma for so many of the families I
coach, and different frames of reference can lead to hard feelings
among siblings. We don't always understand how our brothers and
sisters make decisions. It's easy to believe we will all think alike and
act the same, at least when it comes to major family issues. But, in
fact, our brothers and sisters make decisions differently. We have to
accept them, regardless of the stress this can cause when we're taking
care of our parents.

And we must recognize how many unknown factors can scramble
a situation that seems clear and calm one moment, a crisis the next.
For example, there's the health of your other parent. One night, after
my Mom had been in the hospital and come home, my Dad came
into my room about two in the morning complaining of chest pains.
My sister had gone home to be with her family that night, so I stayed
with Mom while Dad drove himself to the emergency room. (I know,
that sounds crazy – and dangerous. But Dad's family has a hereditary
stubborn streak about three times the width of their backbones, and
he was off before I could get out of bed.)

It turned out to be anxiety, but it threw us for a loop – we'd been
so focused on my Mom's care, we forgot about Dad's tendency to
respond to stress with physical ailments of his own. In the end, we
got a good laugh out of it. As Dad said to me later, "The hospital is
my safe place. Besides, they have really good pancakes."

Planning For Harder Times

If you're in the early stages of a caregiving relationship, it probably
feels like you've got all you can handle just coping with the situation

at hand. Nonetheless, when you're updating your siblings on the current situation, find the time to look ahead. It's hard to spend time before a crisis, looking at all the angles, making flexible plans, and anticipating how we'll need to adjust our lives even more to make caregiving fit. It's rare that we think about what kind of caregiver we want to be, and actively look for help and support for ourselves as well as our parents. But it's extremely important. Otherwise, you're suddenly up to your elbows in alligators and don't know how to back out without consequences.

Every family is different, which means every caregiving situation brings with it unique emotional baggage. But some aspects are predictable, and the pressure this new role will bring to bear on all the other relationships in your life is prominent among them.

So don't lose yourself. Examine your motivation: Why are you thinking of doing this? Are you entering into a caregiving role because you choose to? Or do you feel it's your duty? Are you being "guilted" into it? Is there no one else willing or able? Are you letting long-past sibling rivalries influence your decisions, perhaps to everyone's detriment?

Be smart about the caregiving choices you make. Explore your reasons. Know your limits – and respect them. Enlist help when you need it. Get advice. Learn to say no and know when to let go. It may actually be easier for you to say no to your parents than to say no to those voices in your head that constantly whisper, "You're not doing enough. Don't be so selfish. You don't need a night off." Learning and respecting your limits will serve you and your parents well.

And if you're normal, accept that sooner or later you're going to feel that no one really knows, or appreciates, how much you're doing. If you haven't yet, you will. It goes with the territory. But sometimes a sibling will surprise you – in a good way.

I treasure an e-mail I received from my brother Steve in November 2006. "I can feel that you are under new and different stressors than you were before," he wrote. "And I see why. Not that I didn't know. You have always been the one we all count on in the fam[ily]. It's pretty easy for the rest of us to take it for granted that you are going to handle things. You always have. But it must be tiring. You have your life to take care of and dreams you want to achieve. I am thinking about all this and will try to send you something helpful later. The try part refers to being helpful. Love you – Steve."

Steve's e-mail meant a great deal to me. Too often, caregiving is literally a thankless job. It's amazing how powerful a simple "thanks" or "glad you're there to handle all this" can be, especially when it comes from your parents or your siblings.

Just as caregiving can bring great joy and deepen relationships, it also takes a toll. The key is to be in the driver's seat as much as you can in determining your caregiver role, and accepting – even if you don't always like it – the degree of involvement and support your siblings are able to provide.

Accepting Tough Realities

With my title, I set three goals for this book:

1. To help you keep your parents active: not just busy, but engaged in life, whatever that means for them.

2. To help you keep your parents safe: making smart choices, leading full lives, and feeling secure enough to be willing and able to try new things.

3. To help you keep your parents independent: not that they don't need you, but rather that they remain in charge of those pieces of their lives they can handle while feeling comfortable enough to express what they want and need.

I can't stress enough the importance of being a smart caregiver. Don't enter into this role blindly. The number and sophistication of people and resources available to help you is constantly growing. Just look. And ask.

In particular, take advantage of the mental fitness resources I've listed in the directories that follow: Although not directly linked to the act of caregiving, they can help you become a more flexible thinker, and flexibility is crucial in effective caregiving.

Take care of yourself. It's pointless to exhaust yourself with caregiving, to the point that someone else has to become a caregiver to you. When you feel stuck, or frustrated, pull out a Mental Fitness Card, work a Suduko or dance to the music you love. Get outside of yourself. Laugh, cry and look at your situation from another side.

My Dad always says to me, "Put one thing in front of you and do that." For a multi-tasker like me, that's important – if not always easy – to remember. Otherwise, I'm off trying to handle so many different issues at once that I forget what life is fully about.

Your caregiving role is about making right by mom and dad (and your siblings), about considering the infinite range of possibilities and responses – from the realistic to the absurd – and finally, about letting go and experiencing the process, living the journey. Know that being intentional in your living is better. Holding the hand of mystery and wonder as you journey in love and care with your family is what each of us is called to do.

Get about the business of your life.

ACKNOWLEDGMENTS

There are countless people to thank. The journey that I have taken – of which this book represents just a portion – was rarely taken alone. Audiences everywhere have shared their caregiving stories. My private clients have taught me much about caregiving. And my family has given me ample opportunity to be a caregiver.

Mary Anne Clagett and Pegi Schlis of *Creative Forecasting* magazine have given me a forum in which to develop my thoughts. Don Bastian, Herman Jackson and the supportive staff of Attainment Company continue to bring my ideas to fruition – and print. Marge Engelman remains my mentor and friend, tirelessly working to help people of all ages improve their mental fitness.

The idea for this book was one of those "ah-ha" moments over coffee and conversation with Dick Schaaf. Our partnership with Dick has been tremendous. He is both a talented wordsmith and editor, and just a whole lot of fun to work with. Kirsten Ford provided more than good design; she supplied us with good coffee and cookies during meetings.

Eric Ramlo, my partner in life and work, has been my steady companion and one heck of a copy editor. And there whenever I – knowingly or not – needed a few moments to explore my thoughts and regroup, was Eli, our dog, ever ready to play, cuddle and go for a good hike.

RESOURCES FROM ATTAINMENT

Since its founding in 1979, Attainment Company, Inc., of Verona, Wisconsin, has specialized in creating quality products for people with disabilities and special needs. Product areas include: assistive technology and communication; professional and parent resources; math, literacy and reading; life skills; study aids and accessories; and Individualized Education Program (IEP) resources.

Recently, Attainment began offering resources for older adults. Most of these are targeted for professional use, but I've recommended them to many nonprofessional caregivers who have found them invaluable. All are published by Attainment and are available at the company's website: www.AttainmentCompany.com.

Where I've referenced an item in text, you'll find a numbered symbol ● in front of the listing with a page number keyed to the first or main reference. To find a continually updated directory of resources, please go to www.KariBerit.com and click on the Resources link.

44 *Aerobics of the Mind* (1996)
Marge Engelman, Ph.D.

Aerobics of the Mind DVD (2006)
Marge Engelman, Ph.D., and Kari Berit Gustafson, MS
  Presents the research underpinnings of mental activity for adults and shows how to run a group session on mental fitness.

Memory Tips (2006)
Shelley Peterman Schwarz
  Hundreds of tips and techniques for professional and family caregivers as well as the general population.

46 *Mental Fitness Cards* (2004)
Marge Engelman, Ph.D.

> Provides adults with 100 stimulating brain exercises. Use them one-on-one, with groups, or to get yourself out of ruts!

Mental Fitness DVD (2006)
Based on the work of Marge Engelman, Ph.D., and Kari Berit Gustafson, MS

> Two older adults present 24 mental fitness workouts designed for individuals or groups.

Mental Fitness Instructor's Guide (2005)
Kari Berit Gustafson, MS

> Eight themed mental fitness workouts: Everything you need to run a mental fitness exercise program at your church, with your friends, staff, senior centers, assisted living, etc.; easy to use for participants who vary in ability.

Mind Your Mind (2005)
Beatrice Seagull

> Challenging exercises that sharpen mental prowess in memory skills, flexible thinking, perception, reasoning and more.

Resources on Alzheimer's Disease (2006)
Gail Petersen, Ph.D., and Kim Petersen, MD

> Workbook containing critical information, valuable assessment tools and reproducible in-service handouts for professionals. I've used this with church groups, nursing assistants and the general public to provide valuable information on the various dementias.

Thinking Cards (2004)
Marge Engelman, Ph.D., Danielle Leuthje, MSSW, Gail Petersen, Ph.D., and Kim Petersen, MD

> Similar to Mental Fitness Cards, but adapted for those with Mild Cognitive Impairment (MCI), these cards have a picture on one side and a related exercise on the other. The picture side stimulates a conversation if the written exercise is too difficult.

What Every Caregiver Needs to Know About Alzheimer's Disease DVD (2006)
Gail Petersen, Ph.D., and Kim Petersen, MD
Video-based teaching tool for professional and family caregivers portraying individuals at various stages of Alzheimer's; includes the Resources on Alzheimer's Disease workbook.

Whole Brain Workouts (2006)
Marge Engelman, Ph.D.
124 fun and challenging workouts that apply what research shows keeps the brain healthy.

Books, Organizations And Websites

In addition to resources from Attainment Company, a growing spectrum of books (including children's books), organizations and websites is available to help you in your caregiving. The directory that follows is only a small sampling. In some cases, I've added a specific recommendation based on my own experience. Where I've referenced an item in text, you'll find a numbered symbol ⬤ in front of the listing with a page number keyed to the first such reference. To find an updated directory of resources, please go to www.KariBerit.com and click on the Resources link.

Books

Ageless Spirit, The, 2nd Edition: Reflections on Living Life to the Fullest in Midlife and the Years Beyond, Connie Goldman; Fairview Press (2004).

Aging: The Fulfillment of Life, Henri J.M. Nouwen and Walter J. Gaffney; photographs by Ron P. van den Bosch; Image (1976).
    One of my favorite books on aging.

And Thou Shalt Honor: The Caregiver's Companion, Beth Witrogen McLeod; Rodale Books (2003).
    A touching caregiver's guide that also is filled with information on the basics.

Brain Health and Wellness, Dr. Paul Nussbaum; Word Association (2003).

Paul has it right on when it comes to brain health: The diseases of old age actually begin in childhood, when failure to actively exercise the brain creates the conditions for later brain debilitation. Nussbaum, a licensed clinical neuropsychologist, has more than 15 years' experience in the care of older persons suffering from dementia and related disorders.

Comfort and Be Comforted: Reflections for Caregivers, Pat Samples; ACTA Publications (2003).

Creating Moments of Joy, Jolene Brackey; Purdue University Press (2003).
    If you have a parent with an Alzheimer's-type dementia, Jolene's book is a treasure. Easy to read; easy-to-use suggestions.

57 *Eat Mangoes Naked: Finding Pleasure Everywhere (and dancing with the Pits)*, SARK; Simon & Schuster (2001).

91 *Elements of Mentoring, The*, W. Brad Johnson and Charles R. Ridley; Palgrave Macmillan (2004).

Gifts of Caregiving, The: Stories of Hardship, Hope, and Healing, Connie Goldman; Fairview Press (2002).

Grace Disguised, A: How the Soul Grows through Loss, Jerry Sittser; Zondervan (2005).

47 *Grow Dendrites Forever: 1998 Brain Fitness Kit*, Cynthia S. Short; Cynorge (1997).

Healthy Aging: A Lifelong Guide to Your Physical and Spiritual Well-being, Andrew Weil, M.D.; Alfred A. Knopf (2005).

House of Belonging, The, David Whyte; Many Rivers Press (1996).

How Then, Shall We Live?: Four Simple Questions That Reveal the Beauty and Meaning of Our Lives, Wayne Muller; Bantam (1997).

A wonderful book that guides you in asking some of life's tougher and more important questions.

How to Care for Aging Parents, Virginia Morris; Workman Publishing Company (2004).
One of my favorite guides; covers most of the nitty-gritty basics of providing care to aging parents.

I Only Say This Because I Love You: Talking to Your Parents, Partner, Sibs, and Kids When You're All Adults, Deborah Tannen; Ballantine Books (2002).

I Remember When: Activities to Help People Reminisce, Howard Thorsheim, Bruce Roberts; Elder Books (2000).
Great book with easy-to-use ideas to help you encourage your parents to share stories.

Late-Life Love: Romance and New Relationships in Later Years, Connie Goldman; Fairview Press (2006).
If you're like me, I sort of flipped out when my Dad decided to date again. Books on later love can help you, as well as your parent.

Marketing to Leading-Edge Baby Boomers: Perceptions, Principles, Practices & Predictions, Brent Green; Paramount Market Publishing, Inc. (2006).

20 *New Passages*, Gail Sheehy; Random House (1995).

Open Mind, Open Heart: The Contemplative Dimension of the Gospel, Thomas Keating; Continuum International Publishing Group (1994).

24 *Oxford Book of Aging, The*, Thomas R. Cole, Mary G. Winkler; Oxford University Press (1994).

Places That Scare You, The: A Guide to Fearlessness in Difficult Times, Pema Chödrön; Shambhala (2005).
A book full of wisdom that helps you confront those voices in your head that hold you back.

Reminiscing Together: Ways to Help Us Keep Mentally Fit As We Grow Older, Howard Thorsheim, Bruce Roberts; Compcare Publications (1990).

109 *Secret Power of Music, The*, David Tame; Destiny Books (1984).

Self-Care for Caregivers: A Twelve Step Approach, Pat Samples, Diane Larsen, Marvin Larsen; Hazelden (2000).

Simple Abundance: A Daybook of Comfort and Joy, Sarah Ban Breathnach; Warner Books (1995).

48 *Ten Poems to Change Your Life*, Roger Housden; Harmony (2001).

Ten Poems to Last a Lifetime, Roger Housden; Harmony (2004).

Ten Poems to Set You Free, Roger Housden; Harmony (2003).
   Of all the poetry anthologies out there, Roger Housden's are my favorites. As you read the poems, he acts as your mentor and guide. If you've ever struggled with poetry, Housden will gently guide you through this rich form of writing.

105 *Travel Book, The: A Journey Through Every Country in the World*, Lonely Planet (2005).

Tuesdays with Morrie: An Old Man, a Young Man, and Life's Greatest Lesson, Mitch Albom; Doubleday (1997).

Validation Breakthrough: Simple Techniques for Communicating with People with Alzheimer's-Type Dementia, Naomi Feil; Health Professions Press (1993).
   A fantastic approach to getting into your care receiver's reality.

Wisdom Distilled from the Daily: Living the Rule of St. Benedict Today, Joan Chittister; Harper San Francisco (1991).

Children's Books

37 *Annie and the Old One*, Miska Miles; illustrated by Peter Parnall; Little, Brown (1971).

89 *Charlotte's Web*, E.B. White; Harper & Row (1952).

33 *Giving Tree, The*, Shel Silverstein; HarperCollins (1964).

118 *Lorax, The*, Dr. Suess; Random House (1971).

118 *Keeping Quilt, The*, Patricia Polacco; Simon & Schuster (1998).

35 *Miss Rumphius*, Barbara Cooney; Puffin (1985) or Viking Juvenile (1982).

34 *Old Turtle*, Douglas Wood; watercolors by Cheng-Khee Chee; Scholastic Books (1992).

36 *Old Woman Who Named Things, The*, Cynthia Rylant; illustrated by Kathryn Brown; Harcourt Brace (1996).

118 *Sofia and the Heartmender*, Marie Olofsdotter; Holy Cow! (2007).

118 *Wilfrid Gordon McDonald Partridge*, Mem Fox; illustrated by Julie Vivas; Kane/Miller Book Publishers (1989).

Organizations

AARP: 888/687-2277 or www.aarp.org

49 **Alzheimer's Association:** 800/272-3900 or www.alz.org.

107 **American Music Therapy Association:** 301/589-3300 or www.musictherapy.org.

131 **American Society on Aging:** 800/537-9728 or www.asaging.org.

78 **Concordia Language Villages:** 800/222-4750 or www.concordialanguagevillages.org.

78 **Elderhostel:** 800/454-5768 or www.elderhostel.com.

International Council on Active Aging: 866/335-9777 or www.icaa.cc. Provides education, information, resources and tools for professionals in the retirement, assisted living, fitness, rehabilitation, and wellness fields.

National Council on Aging: 202/479-1200 or www.ncoa.org. The National Council on Aging (NCOA) is dedicated to improving the health and independence of older persons and increasing their continuing contributions to communities, society, and future generations.

130 **Spiritual Directors International:** 425/455-1565 or www.sdiworld.org.

Websites: General

Allen Brain Atlas: www.brain-map.org. To learn more about the human brain, explore this fascinating, interactive, genome-wide image database of gene expression in the mouse brain.

49 **Alzheimer's Association:** www.alz.org.

American Institute of Philanthropy: www.charitywatch.org. A nonprofit charity watchdog and information service.

107 **American Music Therapy Association:** www.musictherapy.org.

131 **American Society on Aging:** www.asaging.org.

AnnualCreditReport.com: www.annualcreditreport.com.

CarePages: www.carepages.com.
   Easy-to-use site that helps family and friends communicate when a
   loved one is receiving care. It takes just a few minutes to create a
   CarePage, share it with friends and family, and build a community
   of support.

Consumer Action Website: www.consumeraction.gov.
   An online consumer guide.

Creating Keepsakes: www.creatingkeepsakes.com.
   You can find anything here from idea pages to quotes for any topic.

Creative Scrapbooking: www.creativescrapbooking.com.
   Shows how to create memory books.

Elder Care Locator: www.eldercare.gov.
   A place to find community assistance for seniors.

Equifax, credit bureau: www.equifax.com.

Experian, credit bureau: www.experian.com.

Federal Trade Commission: www.ftc.gov.
   Agency charged with protecting America's consumers.

Guide to Community Preventive Services:
www.thecommunityguide.org.
   Evidence-based recommendations on public health interventions
   to reduce illness, disability, premature death, and environmental
   hazards that impair community health and quality of life.

55 Helpguide: www.helpguide.org.
   Promotes healthy, active lifestyles.

International Council on Active Aging: www.icaa.cc.

Internet ScamBusters: www.scambusters.org.

102 It's Never 2 Late: www.IN2L.com

138 LifeBio: www.lifebio.com

Centers for Disease Control and Prevention's Healthy Aging website: www.cdc.gov/aging/
> Includes health information for older adults, statistics and research, publications, links to relevant organizations, free subscription to CDC's Healthy Aging ListServe, and more.

National Do Not Call Registry: www.donotcall.gov.

National Council on Aging: www.ncoa.org.

20 Pontell, Jonathan: www.jonathanpontell.com.
> A cultural historian.

57 SARK: www.planetsark.com.
> Author and creativity wiz.

Scrapbook Town: www.scrapbooktown.com.

***Share Your Life with Me Parent Journals*, Linkages & Shoestrings:** www.mymemoryjournals.com/parent_journal.shtml.
> I gave my Dad "Dad, Share Your Life With Me…" one Christmas and asked that he fill it out and return it to me the next year. It is a short journal, asking your parent to answer one question per day. Dad and I talked about this book throughout the year. (I would ask, "How are you doing with your homework?") I treasure the book he returned to me and learned a great deal about my Dad.

130 Spiritual Directors International: www.sdiworld.org.

73 Story Circle Network: www.storycircle.org.

72 **Story Circles International:** www.storycirclesinternational.com.

Today's Caregiver, **magazine:** www.caregiver.com.

TransUnion, credit bureau: www.transunion.com.

U.S. government's consumer web portal: www.consumer.gov.

146 *Who Gets Grandma's Yellow Pie Plate?* **University of Minnesota Extension Service:**
www.extension.umn.edu/info-u/finances/BF840.html.
   A wonderful resource for adult children and parents to use in discussing the passing on of personal possessions.

138 **Your Life Is Your Story:** www.your-life-your-story.com.

Websites: Travel

Armchair Travel: www.armchair.com.

Best Fares: www.bestfares.com.

Cheap Tickets: www.cheaptickets.com.

Digital City: www.digitalcity.com.

78 **Elderhostel:** www.elderhostel.com.

11th Hour: www.11thhourvacations.com.

Expedia: www.expedia.com.

Fodor's: www.fodors.com/miniguides.

Generous Adventures Travel Auctions:
www.generousadventures.com.

Magellan's: www.magellans.com.

Orbitz: www.orbitz.com.

Travelocity: www.travelocity.com.

TravelSmith: www.travelsmith.com.

INDEX